AMRAPALI

AMRAPALI

V Balakrishnan

ZERO DEGREE PUBLISHING

Title: Amrapali
Author's name: V Balakrishnan

Published By: Zero Degree Publishing

Zero Degree Publishing
No. 55(7), R Block, 6th Avenue,
Anna Nagar West,
Chennai - 600040
Ph: 8925061999

E mail: zerodegreepublishing@gmail.com
Website: www. zerodegreepublishing.com
Printed at Manipal Technologies, India.

First Edition by Zero Degree Publishing: March 2023
ISBN: 978-81-949734-3-0
ZDP Title: 54

Cover Design: Meera Sitaraman
Cover Photo: C Vishwajith

Typeset: Vidhya Velayudham
Printed at Clictoprint, India

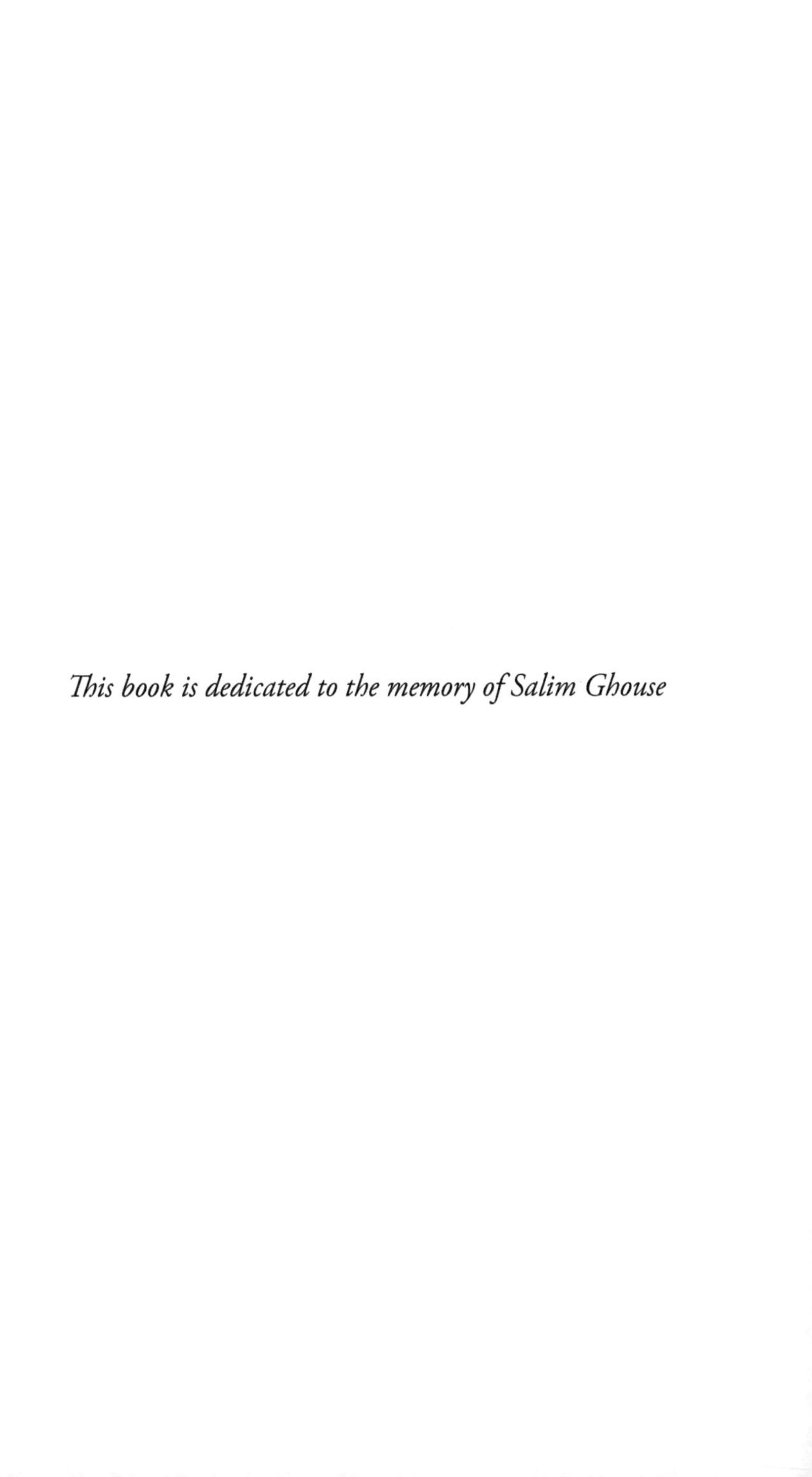

This book is dedicated to the memory of Salim Ghouse

Inspired by

Vaishali ki Nagarvadhu by Acharya Chatursen
Ambapali by Vimala Raina

This is a work of fiction.

The play was first performed in March 2015 at the Alliance Française of Madras with the following cast and crew:

Actor: Janani Narasimhan

Music and Vocals: Nithya Sivashankar

Design and Direction: V Balakrishnan

Photographs are from the performance at Alliance Française of Madras.

Photographs: C Vishwajith, M Sivanesan

Introduction

In the Indian chapter of the Royal Court Theatre's workshop for directors and playwrights (Bangalore 2001), facilitator Ramin Gray educated us that a playwright is a person who makes plays, and not writes them (the word 'wright' being old English for a craftsperson or builder, e.g., wheelwright, cartwright). Till then, I was convinced that this seemingly tough work of creativity required astute knowledge of grammar and sentence formation. After returning from the London chapter of the RCT residency (having attended sessions by Martin Crimp, Caryl Churchill and so many other fascinating makers of plays), I decided to attempt to make a play. My endeavours slowly revealed to me that it was not unlike the process I followed as an actor to facilitate the illusion of a character in the minds of my audience. The task was bare open in its demand. I had to be intuitive in my writing—no forced flowery language, no showing off, but honest, truthful and organic writing. My first calling has always been that of an actor, the facilitator of the illusion, the magician. I became a director out of compulsion (no one was casting me), and now I wanted to make plays that I wanted to articulate on stage. History, legends and myths were my sources of nourishment, feeding my daydreams and imagination, and subsequently providing the building blocks for my plays. (Later, I did make plays like *Sordid*, *Margazhi*, *God's Will* and *Glue*, which came from my present interactions with life.)

How I responded to myths and legends became my plays. How I daydreamed about people from history became my plays. How I sought liberation through these role-plays became my plays. *Amrapali* is one of my most performed plays, and Janani Narasimhan revelled in playing it. I am satiated in the knowledge that this play has stood the test of an audience ample times before coming out as a published play. I mean, what is the purpose of a play but to be performed. If they get published as well, it's nice. For this, I would like to thank my dear friend Nandini Krishnan (a fascinating writer and maker of plays) who trusts my words and what they generate.

V Balakrishnan
October 2022

1

From Muzaffarpur, towards the west,
if you travel hard and long
for 18 miles,
you will come to the town of Vaisaud.
Not much to look at,
a few huts, dung heaps, maybe a dog.
And yes,
people. Lots of people.
Now, if you decide to not let the stench bother you
and look further, squinting your eyes,
you will see old forts and statues,
wasted away by the sun and time.
A faint suspicion
will curl into a smile on your lips—
of a grand city.
A flourishing grandeur of riches and bounty.
Honest truth?
Yes, a city did exist in these parts.
Imposing and famous.
Its name was Vaishali.

7777 palaces,
7777 rest houses,
7777 lakes,
7777 domes.
Unlimited splendour,
unparalleled wonder.
The capital of the Vajji conglomerate.
The capital of the valiant Licchavis.
The treaty of the eight:
Videha,
Licchavi,
Kshatrik,
Vajji,
Ugra,
Bhoja,
Ikshvaku,
Kuru.
The first republic—the first Ganatantra.
Gana, or the people;
Tantra, or action by the people.
As I have laid the foundations of excitement,
of history, of mythology and achievement,
let me introduce the main players:
Bimbisara of Magadha,
Prasenajit of Kosala,

Udayan of Kaushambi,
Chetak of the Licchavis.
No, these are not the main players.
I am sorry. I apologize.
These are mere chapter titles.
Only two main players—
I and another.
Now I can begin my story.
As in, the story belongs to me and it is about me.
A bit of both.
And to begin, I must return.
To take you further into my tale,
I must go back.
Come with me, for relentless time does not wait,
but it affords us to percolate
through the memories and dreams of mine.

2

In the early hours of the morning,
a man—his name is Mahanaman—
walks into the state gardens of Vaishali
to tend the plants and enjoy a private moment
with his dear mango groves.
A bundle catches his eyes
under a mango tree,
almost under her protection.
She stands guard over her precious charge.
Recognizing her gardener, she relinquishes.
Her branches sigh
and swish.
And Mahanaman holds in his hand
a baby, alive.
His palms adorn
a tiny girl,
a newborn.
Must be some apsara[1] who has
abandoned the baby after a risqué jaunt

1 Celestial nymph.

with some mighty sage.
For apsaras do not yield milk.
Their breasts are only for decoration,
for distraction,
for embellishment.
Only the humans can feed their young ones.
The gardener had not beheld
such a bountiful yield in his groves and gardens.
This child, he decides, is his.
And he will be her father.
There is no clue of her lineage or her wretched
parents.
Not a scrap to suggest the origin of this malcontent.
He decides to call her Ambapali—
the daughter of the mango tree.

11 years pass.

The sapling is a plant now,
heartachingly beautiful.
The father has seen the fate
of beautiful women in his city.
Stolen to be sold, coerced to be brides.
And the ancient law:
a girl of extraordinary beauty

must pass life as the State's bride.
Equal rights, every citizen would have on her.
The goddess of the republic: Janapada Kalyani.
How long in seclusion will the gem be hidden?
How long the diamond in the purse?
How long will the fruit be forbidden
to the hungry youth's curse?
Adolescence stretched the fabric of humility
and burst open like a ripe pomegranate.
Ambapali was no longer
a secret, a gardener's daughter.
She was a ravishing, bewitching beauty.
And Mahanaman was summoned to answer
the call of the Clan of Eight.

3

In the parliament of the 999, arose
the Chief.
"Brothers, we have assembled here today
with a singular agenda.
Mahanaman's daughter, Ambapali, has seen 18
summers,
and has been chosen
as a woman of unfathomable beauty.
By the laws of the Republic,
the assembly wishes
to honour her as the Bride of the State.
Bestow upon her, the title of Janapada Kalyani.
Father of Ambapali, do you consent?"
My father arose with dignity
and spoke soothingly,
"Gentlemen, I am a Licchavi...
and for 42 years
my sword-arm has served this assembly
to protect her cause and clause.

M Sivanesan

And then I tended the gardens, never broke the laws.
But as accurately pointed out,
Ambapali has completed 18 years,
and by the laws of our sacred forefathers,
she is free
to make her own decisions.
Let my daughter choose her own destiny."

The young, the youth, the nobles of the state
could not bear a gardener speak up to them,
explain their laws and their intricacies.
They shouted, "Treachery, treachery…
punish this man. The council must uphold the law,
and the law is supreme. Ambapali is the state's
possession."

Seeing my father being bullied,
I stepped out from the crowd, where the
common people congregate
to watch the assembly scream, govern and shout.

There was silence.

Everyone was quiet.

The Vajji council was watching me,
seizing me, and already
very much in love with me.
I spoke,
"Gentlemen, I have pondered hard over your orders.
Either I become the State's property or face death.
This despicable law
is a blemish on our republic.
What is my crime?
That I have been born with a form
that you find irresistible?
And for this crime,
I have to render my life
in a cauldron of insults and shame?
I will lose my rights over my womanhood.
Not allowed to love and live as I choose,
but sit in the open market
and be bidden on by anyone who has a few gold coins.
This law that forces me to bend
to this course of life
is a million times despicable.
You offer me slavery or death.
I don't want to die. Not so soon.
So, I accept the title of the State's Bride.

But, I have a few conditions.
Fulfil them, and take
my womanhood, respect, youth, beauty and this body.
Let your vile and base laws rule."

4

The Kuru youngsters,
the sweet, adorable boys,
new entries to the council,
some by inheritance, some by birth,
with new armour, fresh clothes, and long swords,
rallied and shouted,
"Who dares to force Ambapali to become the State's Bride?
We will soak him in his own blood.
Council of Vajji,
choose the harlots in the market to please your lust.
Do not debase this woman.
Is womanhood so cheap here?
This is an insult.
Destroy the Republic.
Long live Ambapali."

Boys will be boys.
The council elder had to but glare,
and they quieted down

after their vocal attempts to catch my attention
and assert their presence,
in its victorious resonance,
caught the entire assembly's consideration.

Silence followed brash bravery.
War pensions, the warriors' salaries
took precedence.

The elder stood and said,
"Ambapali, quote your wants.
Young men of this assembly,
we will be happy to see
those long swords of yours
being drawn with equal aplomb
very soon, when we will inevitably face
the monster of Magadha,
of the Shishunaga race.
For now, keep them sheathed.
Please, gentlemen, take your seats.
Yes, Ambapali, speak.
What are your conditions?"

999 pairs of eyes were on me.
I had decided to hit them where it hurts.

Make them pay the full price.
"My first condition: I want the woods
where the seven groves exist,
with their lands, animals, air, and water.
I want nine-crore gold coins for their upkeep,
and my house, the State will maintain
like the palace of a royal woman."

"Excellent joke, you bemuse us.
You want the groves of unparalleled splendour,
of mystic and magical wonders?
And that much of gold, I believe,
is the nation's wealth of ten years."

"Give her, elders, give her the gold,
the land, the forest, and the groves.
Empty the treasury. It can be refilled.
Elders, look at us, we are being killed
by the darts of love and amour.
Ambapali, why nine, take a 100-crore."

Pleasures of the flesh, which they envisaged in my
arms, gave their tongues voice.
They grew louder and louder.
And my first condition was passed by the council

without a murmur.
"Elders, listen well, and know my second condition.
My palace is to be protected with soldiers, arms
and a moat.
Ramparts, watchtowers and a solid granite fort.
My guests will be free to come and go.
No scrutiny, no frisking and checks by the security.
Do you agree?"

"No no no, that would be suicide. That is insane.
You could raise your own army and be our bane.
A nest her house will be for traitors and spies,
and gather the best of our enemies—
to savour her pleasures, and wine, and food,
and then hatch Vaishali's doom with intrigue."

"No, elders, never. This will not be agreed upon.
These foolish old men of Vaishali are envious.
Unable to enjoy the pleasures of the flesh,
they wish to deprive us youth of our meat and hunt.
For a woman like Ambapali, this is a choice affront.
Ambe, we agree to grant you an impregnable fort
and our personal soldiers for your escort.
But the men from foreign lands
who wish to enter your realms…

they must be frisked and checked, and will be too.
Relent, Ambapali, mistress of the seven woods
and our hearts.
Let us agree to the deal made, dissolve the assembly
and depart.
Janapada Kalyani, Ambapali, jayatu jayatu[2]!"

Janapada Kalyani—the goddess of the Republic, the
State's whore would be closer.
A price tag fixed on my body: seven groves, palaces
and a fort, and gold.
I did what no ideology could do,
neither religion nor laws could do.
I united the men of the Republic.
I embraced their law and became their asset.
No more a woman ordinary,
no more a common gardener's daughter.
This you see in front of you is Devi Ambapali,
Janapada Kalyani.

My father gently placed me on his lap,
and the nobles poured water on his hands.
The gift of the mango tree

---

2 Goddess of the Republic, Amrapali, may you be victorious, may you be victorious!

was meant to be
the Bride of the State.
Destiny had lost to fate.

5

Everyone has seen the domes, the rest houses,
the taverns, and the slave market of Vaishali.
But not many have seen the holy lake within the city.
The famed, fabled Mangalapushkarani.
Some say it leads to the Nagaloka[3],
while others call it the Lake of Salvation.
I looked at it and knew what it was—an ordinary lake
with an extraordinary reputation.
The Licchavi nobles held the exclusive permission
to sport in this lake.

No one else, not even their wives or children
were allowed to step in.
Eunuchs bearing naked swords guarded this lake.
I was led into it and I stood in the horribly cold water.
My clothes dripping, my flesh shivering,
and I was sworn in
as an honorary council member.

---

3 The deepest realm in Hindu cosmology after Svarga (Heaven) and Prithvi (Earth) and also considered the abode of snakes.

“I, Devi Ambapali, belong to the Republic of Vaishali.
I, Devi Ambapali, will obey and respect the 7 rules of
the Licchavis.”

“By the order of the Republic of the Vajjis,
by the protection of the eight clans,
I present to you Janapada Kalyani—Devi Ambapali.”

And it was over.

6

The seven woods, my new home.
It had seven grounds.
The first was a parking lot for all the chariots,
elephants, palanquins, and horses.
The second hosted my personal army, and animals—
exotic birds and beasts.
Gifts from kings, princes, and merchants
from China, Burma, Swarnadweepa, Singhala, and
Kambhoja.
The third, my personal artists' conservatory,
where they sculpted, moulded, painted, and crafted
images of me,
in poses of dance.
The fourth, my factory of perfumes and delicacies.
The fifth, guarded by the eunuchs, my treasury.
The sixth, the house of entertainment
where I received all the young men
who had no second thoughts about losing their hearts,
wealth, and luck to me; to dice, to dance, and music.

And the seventh, my residence, where no one was allowed.

Men came, drank, gambled, loved and lost.
I had slaves who helped me entertain them.
Sometimes the men tried to molest the maids.
They found them easy pickings.
Slaves, you see,
bought from the market.
Most were gifts—gifts from mothers to their newly wed daughters,
who sold them to traders
before their husbands misplaced their eyes.
Gifts from fathers to their sons,
who sold them to traders
fearing their lovers' war cries.
Gifts from kshatriyas to brahmanas.
And the twice-born, in the market, sold,
with no compunction,
weeping little girls for gold.
I chanced upon the slave market when I was riding my chariot in the early hours of Ekadashi.[4]
From 12 to 30,
women from everywhere.

---

4 11th day after a new moon or a full moon.

From raids, from lands foreign and neighbouring.
A father down on bad times,
a husband down on bad debts,
a bet lost, a silent crime;
yesterday a princess, today a slave.

Men would run their fingers
in the slaves' mouths
to test their teeth,
and wipe their hands across the slaves' faces.
Weigh and crush their breasts
to test their flesh.
Pinch their thighs.
Run their fingers between their legs
to test their virginity,
then haggle with the slave trader.
The deal struck,
and the woman changed hands.

I could not stop the nobles from
groping my slaves, slipping their hands inside their
blouses,
casually, playfully, as if it was the most natural gesture
to violate a woman's privacy,
when she had not any social vesture.

As if plucking a grape and tossing it into their wine-
scented mouths,
as if wiping their brows in a sultry drouth.
For they had gold,
and gold solved everything.
Gold was the cure.
The panacea,
the spell,
the medicine,
the truth,
and when required, the lie,
the grammar, the lexicon, and the why.
And gold was one language
Ambapali spoke effectively.

7

I was not cruel, but a sport.
I was rich and a very good host.
Men were welcomed, and offered drinks and wine,
betel and dry fruits, and music and dance,
and everything to make them feel like gods divine.
The crass and the crude, the boor and the moor,
the ugly and the gods,
all were welcomed and met at the doors,
flirted with, and made to loosen their purse strings,
and by late night, their jewels, gold, bangles and rings.
No man without the door fee could enter,
nor spend a moment in my divine bower.
No money, no honey.
No gold, nothing sold.
A smile was expensive,
so was a kiss.
A song was ransomed,
and a dance was priceless to behold.

One day, a man by sheer madness,

or perhaps the laxity of my guards and servants,
broke into my house.
A handsome poet, poor in riches,
but rich in verses,
came into my entertainment one evening,
flourishing a knife to his chest and cried,
"My heart burns for you. Let me be yours."

I spoke,
"Come to my abode as you please.
Be my lover, if you desire,
but will you be able to sight
the love games I play
with all the men present here?
They will seduce and I will be seduced.
This is a public place.
Please visit when your heart desires.
But please, in robes of silk
and perfumes of Arabia.
This is the abode of the Janapada Kalyani.
Well ornamented,
sprinkling diamonds and pearls,
a smile on your lips,
lust in your eyes.
Come.

Indulge.
Laugh.
Talk.
Pay your bills,
and with an empty heart,
and an emptier purse,
return.
Visit again."

He got up, stared, burst into tears
and was never seen again.

8

My residence was a melting pot
of stories and myths and plots,
of tales of kings and their lives,
of royalty and half-caste wives.
Prasenajit of Kosala,
the dirty old man,
I heard, was in search of a medicine man
who could restore his sexual vigour and give him
strength
to use on all those princesses,
slaves, and all young women.
His son was the angry Vidurath,
who had his father thrown away
and took on the great Kosala and Saket in his royal
sway.
Udayan of Kaushambi, the veena vidwan[5], lover of
Vasavadatta, Sagarika, Padmavati and many more,
kept his distance and watched the plots unfold from

5 Scholar.

the Ganges shore.
Gandhara was subdued by Magadha's might.
I heard whispered a vishkanya[6] was the cause of the blight.
And Magadha, the greatest kingdom of the Mahajanapada,
ruled by the handsome, arrogant king—Bimbisara.

Bimbisara was Vaishali's son-in-law,
but that did not deter him from attacking the Republic.
He had but one ambition—
to rule the entire Jambudweepa
like the erstwhile king of Magadha, Jarasandha.
He attacked our cities… was repulsed.
The Licchavis could lift their swords higher than their wine cups.
The flower garlands my maids placed around their necks
were exchanged for battle armours within moments.
The lure of wine was vanquished
by the lust for war,
as if they commanded it;
in a fraction, demanded it.

6 Refers to a young woman trained to be an assassin.

It was a full moon evening,
and I
was giving a recital to the gathered merchants, nobles,
and warriors,
when we heard the bugle sound thrice.
The Magadhas had landed on boats
in the veil of darkness.
The nobles stood up as one and ran to their carriers.
Within minutes, the town was decorated with
armour-clad warriors.
They rushed into war under the able guidance
of the commander chosen by the council.
The war cry was taken up by all the federations,
the members, and their vassals.

9

The next one week was quiet.
No dance, no love, no wine.
Only news from the battlefield.
Some we lost, others we won.

"Someone was wounded."
"No no, he died."
"Bimbisara has fallen in battle."
"No no, it was his cousin."

News led, mislead, and we only knew
fear and cold dread.
Vaishali was fighting valiantly...
But Bimbisara was a tyrant.
And then, good news—Bimbisara
had vanished like a ghost from the battle scene.
He was nowhere to be seen.
Was he dead or bled?
But no, not so much good fortune.
Just a lucky arrow that struck him

and he removed himself from the battlefield.
The rumour
was that a Kuru arrow had pierced his shoulder
and he had left for Magadha to tend to his serious wound.
The battle raged under the command of Bimbisara's minister—the great Varshakar.
The young prince, Bimbisara's first born,
in the absence of the war lion,
saw this as his opportunity
to glow, to grow, to be the new scion.
He unleashed a wrath that was becoming difficult for the Licchavis to bear.
His name was a travesty.
His name meant 'one without enemies'.
But he was to attract them throughout his life, like fleas.
Without remorse, men and more men he slew.
In his father's absence, the cub made his debut.
The ministers' oily ministrations did ensue.
The good did eschew,
and evil grew,
in the shade of
Ajatashatru.

10

Vaishali was a ghost town.
Not a chariot to be seen on the common roads.
My palace of seven groves was quiet.
It's administration easier, maintenance costly.
I was getting bored without my guests.
I was used to adorations, being pampered, loved,
drenched with pearls and diamonds.
To taste the succulence of exotic fruits from Kashmira
and the lands beyond.
Now, everything was at a premium.
But I missed my dance, music,
and casual flirtations the most.
One night, as I was sitting alone in my chamber,
my maid rushed in to say that a merchant wanted to
be entertained.
I was flabbergasted. This was wartime.
Who had the money to be entertained
by the most expensive courtesan of Jambudweepa?
I had him frisked and searched.
These were difficult times and one had to be careful.

His mudra revealed he was indeed a merchant—
Somadeva from Kaushambi.
But he had a limited purse,
hardly enough to hire me, Ambapali.
I asked my maids to give him some wine,
sweet-talk him,
maybe play a few rolls of dice,
and then get rid of him.
He walked in.
I stared at him…
Such a specimen of manhood
did not exist in Vaishali.
Tall, broad-shouldered, curly hair.
I was yearning for companionship
and here was a man who deserved my company.
Maybe it was my boredom,
but I decided to be his hostess for the night.

But when is the night so alert?
And it seeped into day.
Our treaty was extending its frontiers
but I needed him to pay.
He gave me one ornament from his body every night.
The second night he was
a man… brash and unrestrained. But I did not rush.

My price was a ring.
The third night he was
a poet when he spewed words
to redden my cheeks and make me blush.
My price were his earrings.
The fourth night he was
a warrior. We wrestled
and engaged each other in deadly locks and holds.
My price was an amulet of red gold.
The fifth night
he sang,
and I strummed.
At times, the instrument.
At times, his predicament.
My price was a box made of rare elements.
The sixth night
he played the veena.
The special veena, which Udayan had gifted me,
with seven strings.
And he played and played like a celestial fiend.
And I danced with him, changing tempo and rhythm.
That night he gave me a gift of pink pearls
strung in a necklace.
So precious.
The seventh night

we played dice,
wagered our clothes; we both lost
and we both won.
I had committed a serious felony.
The Janapada Kalyani was supposed to remain a virgin
till
the day a new one was chosen.
But I was not thinking of any consequences,
ramifications.
I had found someone I did not want to let go.

The war was progressing at a ferocious pace
on the borders and at my place. The news was
that the Licchavis were being pushed back
by the armies of Magadha.
And I
was pushing fate.

Bimbisara was healing in Magadha.
I was dying and arising in my lover's arms.

Ajatashatru was indulging in manslaughter, not war.
I was at war; nights were short and days kept them
afar.

It was the eighth night.
Somadeva, my lover,
was looking worried.

"I need to leave, Ambe."

"Why, my love? Are you displeased with me?
Or bored of me?"

"Neither, Ambe."

"Are you out of gold and ornaments to pay me?
Then fear not, my love, for the self, there is no fee."

"No, I have shirked my duty
and staked others to my responsibility.
I have to confess to you.
I have cheated you,
fooled you,
and now I am in love with you."

"So, you have a wife… and children too?
Or are you a dacoit? Or worse still, a deserter?"

"No, Ambe, I am not a dacoit."

"Aha, a deserter."

"Yes, I am."

"Which army?"

"The Magadhan army."

"Aaa, you are an enemy…"

"No, Ambe, I am not.
Listen to me and judge me with a kind eye.
I am not what I seem, my identity was a lie.
I was fighting and slaughtering the Vajjis
without remorse or any emotion.
But one day, in the heat of war,
in the middle of death's dance floor,
I was fighting two Licchavi nobles
at the same time.
I proved to be the better warrior.
I slew one, and then the other.
As his life was leaving his body,
in his dying breath
he said, 'I die with happiness…

But alas… will there be an Ambapali in the warriors' heaven?'
I was amazed that a woman's name a man chose
as life was closing its ornamental doors.
I made enquiries and was astounded by the stories I heard about you.
I wanted to see for myself,
so, I deserted the war and came here,
to you.
And now I am miserably in love with you, Ambe."

"Who are you that have hidden your identity from me?
Who are you if not a merchant trustee?
Who are you that made me agree,
sucked honey like a boisterous bee,
and now claim to be
not what I see?"

"I am Bimbisara."

"It cannot be…
The son-in-law of Vaishali;
the husband to the daughter of the council president;

the king of Magadha—
Bimbisara."

"I ask you right here to become the queen of
Magadha."

"The monster of Magadha…
I gave myself to you?
You bloodthirsty tyrant…
Enemy of my people…
Get out of here
before I call my soldiers
and present your head
to my people.
Leave now.
No, don't speak…
Always a rapist is a stranger…
That's a lie we believe
because the unknown is safer
than the hurt of the known.
You made me, the pride of Vaishali, bow to you.
Ambapali will die than accept this.
Bimbisara… leave… and never return.
And yes, if I meant more than a whore to you—
for the sacred books say that a man who deflowers a

virgin
owes her his responsibility—
stop this war now.
Leave… wretched king…
please go… and remember,
you leave behind a crushed flower."

And that was the first and last time
I had a lover.
Not all the moats, soldiers and fort walls
could withstand the seduction
of the Magadha monster.
He did not defile me, abuse me or force me ever.
But
here I was—violated, deflowered and rubbished.

M Sivanesan

11

I awoke to the sounds of bugles and conch shells.
Licchavi nobles were riding on the streets,
attired in rich gold and silks.
Bimbisara had withdrawn his troops.
The war had been called off.
Ajatashatru had fumed and fretted.
A sure victory was averted
by Bimbisara,
who gave orders, without any preamble,
to withdraw.
The nobles slapped each other's backs
and yapped about their war glories.
Bimbisara was no coward…
that much I knew.
He had called off the war
because I had asked him to.
The price of my virginity
he had paid
without flinching.

The dead were spoken of with reverence.
Many sons and lovers were dead.
Many funeral pyres were lit.
Many a goblet of wine was drunk.
That night, with vengeance, the men returned to my palace.
The men were rowdier than usual.
They drank more, roughened up the maids,
groped the slaves, laughed, and demanded that their needs be fulfilled.
I forgave them.

A few years in peace rolled by.
Bimbisara was imprisoned by his son.
Ajatashatru—the new king of Magadha,
could not wait to let his father
naturally adorn the funeral pyre.
He had him arrested and placed in an eerie dungeon,
left to die by starvation.
Ajatashatru's mother tried to save the emperor
by smearing honey on her body
which he could lick off for sustenance.
Ajatashatru, in retaliation, had his father's Achilles tendons cut.
I had no news of what transpired, but one day,

a merchant told me with conviction—
Bimbisara was dead. Executed by his first born,
Ajatashatru.

His first act on ascending the throne
was to declare war on the Licchavis.
This time he had with him
strange war weapons
one had not heard of:
chemicals, mace swinging tanks, catapults.
Floods in the Ganges stalled his plans.
But the Licchavis had started collecting
along the border.
The call to arms was the Republic's order.
The oath was to finish off Magadha,
once and for all times.

12

King Bimbisara, I heard, had died
with a strange chant on his lips—
"Buddham Saranam Gacchami.
Dhammam Saranam Gacchami.
Sangham Saranam Gacchami."[7]
What did these words mean?
I asked my maid
who had once served in Shravasti
and boasted of knowing eight languages.
She told me a strange story.
"A prince of the Shakya tribe
renounced his house, child and wife,
and in pursuit of foolish whims and mad desires,
that selfish egotist, thousands of acolytes acquires.
Hailed in his crazy kingdom of the wilderness,
with mad power over kings, he preaches forgiveness.
He preaches no salvation for women
and rejects them in his fold.

---

7 I go to Buddha for refuge, I go to the Doctrine for refuge, I go to the Order for refuge

Fears for the longevity of his newfound sect
and the weakness of his acolytes' flesh.
No women, no wine, and absolution.
A fake belief he gives them in redemption.
Spineless worms reject responsibility
and leave their old parents, children to their wives.
And in saffron robes, they feel like saints… The
hypocrites."
I laughed at the venom my maid could spew.
Her man to the Shakyamuni's[8] fold… flew.
And not much I thought of this prince or his shaven
head followers…

Yet, I saw in the faces of the bhikkus[9]—
who, to beg, adorned our doors—
a strange satisfaction, a peaceful contentment.
Not inertia but action; peace, not strife.
Shaven heads and saffron robes were aplenty in
Vaishali.
Men I had entertained and frolicked with
gave up their lands and jewels, wives and golden rules,
and followed the path of the Shakya prince.

---

8 Gautama Buddha.

9 Buddhist monk.

13

Of young men and fighters, there was a dearth.
And Ajatashatru had launched the attack from the Patliputra fort.
The enemy advanced… the enemy was repelled.
Sometimes we shouted in joy and festivity,
and groaned at times in despair and depravity.
The princes, chiefs, and soldiers from the field of battle
threw their turbans and thoughts to the winds.
They lost the desire to think.
They wanted to feel.
Feel happy… Feel sappy.
Feed themselves well… Be comforted and loved.
Live and cram the vestiges of life
in their short spans from the battlefield.
Drunken swagger of swaying soldiers,
reckless vengeful love
demanded from the harlots.
They seemed to be the enemy beneath them…
Such closeness of flesh they had smelt

recently on the battlefield.
Sweat, fluids, blood.
Suddenly they seemed to be the nemesis
and had to be punished.
They became Magadha soldiers in their arms
and suffered their excesses, their crudeness and abuses.
This obscene savagery within the city
grew and threatened.

Every day Ajatashatru advanced,
Vaishali lost its stance.
Vaishali was pushed to the rear.
Vaishali shrank in fear.
Young men ran to become Buddhists,
for it promised them a way
from this continuous strife.
A merchant had an idea…
Why not call the Buddha to our town?
If the enlightened one came to the city,
maybe Ajatashatru could be coerced
to lift the siege and walk away.
A foolish faith of blinded men.
A foolish faith of tired and weary men.
A foolish faith of desperate men.

Relentless time ebbed.

14

And I was reckless and bored.
Upon my chariot I rode,
and
without direction, I rushed.
I was sick of death all around me.
Wounded soldiers whom the Magadha swords fell.
Strange, malaise-ridden soldiers… the chemicals'
perverse spells.
Death everywhere…
I rushed into the streets of my city,
onto the dusty roads,
by the shops of shrouds and funeral attires,
into the womb of the city of 7777 domes,
when I saw a sea of saffron approaching me.
Silent…
without a murmur.
A thousand men or more.
I was incapable of stopping this sea
which was engulfing my city and the country.
So, I stuck to my path.

I will make them give me way.
I will part this fancy new-feigned idea.
I rushed pell-mell into the congregation.

The bhikkus, in fear, moved away from my way…
When suddenly my chariot stopped.
A hand grabbed my bridle and I was roughly blocked.

"Bhikku, why this commotion? Why this anger?
You follow peace and salvation…
Let go of me and my horse… Let us depart."

"Tathagat[10] walks on this path.
It is improper that you will pass
raising dust and disrespect.
Stand aside, and leave once we have left."

"Bhikku, my horse will not know an elevated soul.
His hoofs are trained to kick and trample.
You are too haughty and too loathsome
to dress in saffron robes.
You shun your life and seek salvation…
I live to redeem souls… I am the Janapada Kalyani.
How is your Tathagat superior to me?"

---

10 Another name for the Buddha.

"You who revel in earthly sin
and evoke the unrest of desire
from the spicy wine of your being,
you are the debased mean fire
which burns all goodness within.
The dust of his feet is more sacred than you."

"Brother, do you think you defile me?
No, brother, you reject your own preaching.
I am base and worse than his feet's dust…
But you have defiled the enlightened one's teaching
and succumbed to anger's lust.
See the sky and see it sharp…
See the mists and trace your eyes…
See the dust of the earth
and the horizon where they mingle like lovers spent...
I am the base earth, and he the heaven divine?
But in affinity, I am his, and he is mine.
I excel him, I think, bald acolyte.
Leave my way now… I leave you to your miserable plight."

The crowd parted and the saffron sea divided.
I rode my chariot in the way provided.
And I rode away and crossed half my way

when I know not what happened.
I stopped and slackened.
I descended my chariot and gazed upon a man.
He was no man but a brilliant, luminous sight.
He was energy, he was the cosmos, the ultimate light.
I spoke. I don't know what I said.
But later I was told what was heard—
"I am Ambapali, the nagarvadhu[11] of Vaishali,
and I wish to invite Tathagat and his disciples
to my house for a meal.
And if it be true
what you say,
that all humans are to be treated
equally,
then I consider my invitation accepted."

---

11 Bride of the city.

15

I rushed away having said that and his silent consent
followed me home and to my doors, to my living
room.
I called my maids, my slaves, my friends, and cooks.
"Get a meal ready for a thousand men."

"What to cook, Devi? What kind of men are these?
Red meat, wine and deep-fried boar?
Or berries, vegetables and fruit salads and sauces?
Shall we make them food of aphrodisiac quality?
Or saatvik aahar[12] with roots and fruits in plenty?
Shall we get the Gandhara wines
and China opium to follow?
Or some sherbets and sweeteners and beeda[13] to go?"

All this for any prince will suffice…
And lots of ghee-laden basmati rice.

---

12 Pure and good quality food.

13 A preparation combining betel leaf with areca nut and sometimes tobacco. It is chewed for its stimulant and psychoactive effects.

But he is not a prince of men.
He is the prince of hearts.
What can I offer him who desires nothing?
Yes, I know, I will offer him everything.
We set on to get everything ready
for Tathagat and his followers aplenty.

The Vajji noblemen,
that too not ordinary of might,
stepped in, the lords who formed the Clan of Eight.
"Ambe, we heard you beat us
to inviting the lord for a meal.
Well done, you naughty girl,
but what use to you a holy one's zeal?
Tell you what, love of our life,
sell the opportunity to us for a bag of gold each
and you rejoice in your pleasure house."

"No, it cannot be."

"Ha ha, you are crafty, Ambapali.
Fine. Yes, we agree, we were selling you short.
Ok, listen, a bag of gold each, a litter made of silk,
rubies and diamonds from Golconda,
and three brand new Arabian steeds."

"No, it cannot be."

"Don't anger us, woman.
Withdraw your invite,
and let us play the hosts
to the noble muni[14] and his horde.
You can take all we have said… We will throw in
a little more.
Withdraw now, or face the consequences."

"Gentlemen, the same threat, years ago,
made me relinquish everything I believed in.
In retrospect, I believe, my slender neck
would have preferred the sharp axe
than the arms and slurred speech of drunken men,
their crude advances and dirty pecks.
Kill me if you want… but no,
the honour of serving Tathagat is mine.
Keep your riches, and your gold and your jewels.
I cannot be fooled anymore with stones and rubble.
The lord will eat here, and then this palace of mine,
with the seven groves and all that is mine to commit,
I will lay at the feet of the lord to use and habit.

---

14 Seer.

Nobles, thank you for your patronage, money and its use.
Ambapali resigns from her post of the State's Bride…
And you may choose some other wretched girl as your muse.
Live, and live well in your arrogance and pride."

16

A hidden shaft from my heart was dislodged.
How had I not noticed and felt?
The rubies, diamonds… they smelt
of painful desire, fear and agony.
Is that why I spent life in melancholy?
Had I met the banisher of pain?
I had spoken to the nobles of Vaishali
without planning or thought.
I had no idea my heart had decided
to speak all that I said.
But I felt relieved,
I was joyous.
I had not conceived
that giving up my gold, my lands, my title
would make easier this span of life so brittle.
I was one with the dirt, the air and the sky.
I felt elevated. I was high.

I was free.

I was free earlier from hunger…
Now I was free of being hungry.

I was free earlier from enemies…
Now I was free from hatred.

I was free earlier from poverty…
Now I was free from desires.

I was free earlier from not having a roof…
Now I was free to any tree shade choose.

17

My silky, fragrant hair I cut and presented
to Ajatashatru,
when in triumph he rode into Vaishali.
As he walked in with his naked sword,
I walked out with my staff and bowl.
He walked into darkness and despair;
I walked into glorious light.
He walked into riches, and gold, and jewels;
I walked with the three gems of Buddha's rules.
He walked with the burden of a million deaths;
I walked with the burden of only my robes.

18

I had walked with my naughty gait
and fed man's pride to his full.
Ignorance. Suffering. Desire.
And when his engorged ego could take no more,
I discarded him like a banana peel.
Right belief. Right intent.

I was proud of my beauty,
and prouder of the envious glances
that all women threw at me.
Right speech. Right behaviour.

I pitied none.
But as I kept walking
relentlessly—Right livelihood, Right effort—
I reached the space
beyond the market place
and found peace
under the same tree

where I was found.
Right contemplation. Right concentration.

In the same grove
I was crowned
the Janapada Kalyani, the queen,
who now sits under a tree, by all seen.
No more gifts, adorations or entry fee.
Ambapali was owned by all and now is free.
The daughter of the mango tree
rests under her mother's shade.
My yearnings stilled.
My grief gone.

My heart is now healed.

Epilogue

I flaunted tresses that curled at the ends, resembling
black-bodied bees.
Now, seem like Indian hemp, mangled with time, the
relentless disease.
But, the immutable truth prevails.

I had eyebrows curved to perfection by nature's
flourish;
cascading crinkles, no longer will age nourish.
But, the immutable truth prevails.

Brilliant eyes sparkling like fireflies,
their resplendence now dies.
But, the immutable truth prevails.

Statuesque nose, proud as a mountain peak,
a limp pepper now, forlorn and weak.

But, the immutable truth prevails.

Ears like bracelets well-shaped,
now by time waped.
But, the immutable truth prevails.

My teeth white like snow,
stained and craggy now.
But, the immutable truth prevails.

I crooned like a cuckoo bird,
now my voice like a kettle drum is heard.
But, the immutable truth prevails.

My majestic smooth arms,
with time, wrinkle and deform.
But, the immutable truth prevails.

My rounded uplifted breasts,
now drained of splendour, fallen crests.
But, the immutable truth prevails.

Like polished pure gold my body shone,
now with age, its splendour shorn.
But, the immutable truth prevails.

Strong, smooth thighs I had,
like bamboo, they are knotted and cragged.
But, the immutable truth prevails.

Soft and splendid were my feet,
now crack like earth burnt with heat.
But, the immutable truth prevails.

Once a mansion of glory,
now a forgotten wretched story.
But, the immutable truth prevails.

Such beauty has never been mine before.

M Sivanesan

Photo Credit: M Sivanesan

About the Playwright

V Balakrishnan, an alumnus of Shri Ram Centre for Performing Arts (New Delhi) and the National School of Drama (New Delhi), is the founder and artistic director of Theatre Nisha. He has directed over 210 plays, acted in over 160 plays and written more than 15 scripts.

He was awarded the Charles Wallace Scholarship to attend an International Residency with the Royal Court Theatre, London. In 2017, he was awarded the Fulbright Distinguished Award in Teaching (FDAT). In 2018, the Rotary Club of Madras East conferred the Dronacharya Award on him for his contributions to theatre education. In 2019, he won the Hindu Playwright Award for his script *Sordid* and was chosen as a Fellow for the Arts for Good Fellowship 2019 organised by the Singapore International Foundation. He won the Sultan Padamsee Award for Playwriting 2022 for *God's Will.*

In 2022, Zero Degree Publishing published four of his plays – *The Curse of Urvashi*, *The Peacock Prince*, *Krishna's Dark Son* and *Dvijottama*. Most recently, Dhauli Books has published three of his plays – *Sordid*, *Margazhi* and *Arundhati* – as a collection.

www.ingramcontent.com/pod-product-compliance
Ingram Content Group UK Ltd.
Pitfield, Milton Keynes, MK11 3LW, UK
UKHW041952190726
13854UKWH00005B/1931

Say Yes to the Mess

KIRA ARCHER

This book is a work of fiction. Names, characters, places, and incidents are the product of the author's imagination or are used fictitiously. Any resemblance to actual events, locales, or persons, living or dead, is coincidental.

Kira Archer Books
PO Box 146
Muncy, PA 17756
www.kiraarcherbooks.com

Cover images from Depositphotos
Cover design by Kira Archer

First edition November 2022

For Lisa, without whom I'd still be staring blankly at my
screen in abject terror.
Thank you.
I think...

Chapter 1

Summer Laurent held the engraved silver lighter in her hand, debating the merits of just burning down her house as opposed to trying to sell it.

On one hand, it would feel better than a full body massage whilst laying on a private beach in the tropics on a fur-covered, oversized bean bag stuffed with rainbows to watch the place reduced to nothing but rubble and ash. A definite mark in the pro list.

But she *had* been happy there once. Briefly. So, con? Con-ish, at least.

"Put the lighter down and step away slowly."

Summer glanced at Emily, her BFF since forever, and gave her a wicked little smile. "I wouldn't really do it."

Emily cocked an eyebrow at her. "Uh huh. I can see you making a pro and con list in your head as we speak."

Summer just grinned again. Emily knew her too well. "No worries. So far, the con side is winning. I think."

"Good. I mean, don't get me wrong, the look on Taylor's face would be worth the prison sentence, seriously."

Summer snorted. "True. But..." She sighed and looked around. "I did put a metric shit ton of work into remodeling it. It would be a shame to destroy all that hard work, I suppose."

"Agreed. Add that to the con side. Not to mention this place is a total unicorn. A gorgeous house in a pretty, well-maintained neighborhood—a perfect little slice of suburban pie, I believe you called it—with *no* HOA? Definitely too rare a find to destroy."

"Yeah." Summer pursed her lips. "Plus, the whole 'felony arson' thing. Huge con."

"Also agreed. I look horrible in orange."

Summer sighed again. "Probably best to just let the realtors handle things, I guess."

"Yeah. Despite how amazing it would be to give that ass you divorced the ultimate middle finger," Emily said with a mischievous smile that had Summer laughing.

Watching Taylor's face as his pride and joy burned to the ground? Absolute pro. This house had probably been the only thing Taylor had ever really cared about. Well, not the house but what it represented. Success. Money. Those had been Taylor's main loves in life. Appearances were everything to him, and she'd never quite fallen in line with what he had in mind. Despite every effort she'd made to make his life run as smoothly and perfectly as possible.

Her fingers twitched on the lighter again. She finally put it down on the mantle with a sigh. Who was she kidding? She didn't break the rules. Not anymore, at least. The rulebreaker in her died the day she said "I do" to Taylor. She'd banished any form of mess or chaos in the name of survival. Now she was the queen of rules. Had a whole spreadsheet system of them that governed every aspect of her well-ordered life. She certainly wouldn't break an actual law.

Besides, she needed the money she'd get from the sale. She and Taylor had agreed to sell the house and divide the profits as part of their divorce settlement. And she needed the cash. Her job as a speech therapist at the Academy by the Bay, a private elementary school in the area, was one of the few highlights in her life, but it wouldn't exactly put her in the lap of luxury. And her two-income household had just dropped to one.

There wouldn't be a settlement. Pretty much every dime they'd made had been sunk into the house. An investment for a future that would never happen. Her lawyer had tried to get her to go for alimony, but that would mean keeping Taylor in her life in some capacity and that was too high a price to pay for a little financial security. She was employed, she'd be fine. And the money from the house sale would give her enough cushion not to be in a constant state of panic.

So. No arson...for now. In fact, she should probably do one more walk through and make sure it looked its best.

"Okay," Emily said, hoisting a box into her arms. "This is the last of it. I've got to head over to my sister's and rescue Josh from the kids. You're coming over later, right?"

"Yes, but what about Taylor's box? I told him I'd leave it here so he can get it when he comes by later."

"I sorta forgot that in Josh's truck. But don't worry, I've got someone bringing it over," she said over her shoulder as she headed out the door.

"What? Who?"

"You'll see!"

Emily shoved the box in her back seat and hopped in the car, waving to Summer on her way out of the driveway.

Summer squinted after her friend, not sure if she should be more exasperated or amused. Knowing Emily...exasperation for sure.

She glanced down at her phone. Whoever Emily was sending better hurry. Summer wanted to be out of here before Taylor showed up at six to do his own walk-through. She had over an hour before he was supposed to show, but she wanted to get out with plenty of time to spare. The last thing she wanted was to run into him. Hence the scheduled times for them each to do a last pass through the house.

She was pretty sure he'd purposely left his junk mixed in with her belongings just so they'd have to see each other again. He seemed to delight in rubbing his newfound freedom in her face. Like she'd been keeping him captive since college. If she'd thought he'd been even half as miserable as she'd been, she would have happily divorced him a long time ago instead of trying to make it work for his sake. Before he'd had the time to completely demoralize her.

Twenty minutes later, and Summer was still waiting. She checked her phone again, then sent a quick text to Emily.

Summer: *So where is this person? I want to be gone before HE shows up.*

Emily texted back almost immediately.

Emily: *He got lost but should be there any second.*

Summer*: He???*

Emily*: You can thank me later.*

Summer: *Um, okay?*

Emily: *In fact, I'll just say you're welcome now.*

Summer rolled her eyes.

Summer: *I love you lady but you are one odd fuck.*

Summer gasped. Freaking autocorrect!

Summer: *Oh shit! I meant DUCK. One odd duck!*

Emily: *Ha! Yeah right. I mean both are pretty accurate. So I've been told.*

Summer: *Omg I don't want the details.*

Emily: *Eh, you've heard them all before anyway.*

Summer: *I'm going now. Love you.*

Emily: *Right back atcha babe.*

Summer chuckled and took a deep breath, looking around her. She turned in a slow circle, saying a last goodbye to the home she'd expected to spend the rest of her life in. The modern, open floor plan with its massive great room, fully modern kitchen, clean lines, and nearly colorless palette wasn't truly her dream house. Every choice had been a compromise with Taylor. And while she'd thought she'd been happy with the final result, it just now hit her how much of her own preferences she'd really conceded. In fact, looking at the stark, blank walls, she had a hard time remembering just which parts of the house had been her choice at all.

Yet another monument to how much she'd given up trying to make someone else happy.

And that thought made it much easier to walk away from it all.

She smiled and sucked in a deep breath, her body nearly thrumming with adrenaline at the new life that was laid out before her. Was some of that adrenaline sheer and utter terror? Abso-fucking-lutely. But there was excitement in there too. A sense of adventure that she wasn't usually comfortable feeling. But right now...it felt amazing. She was going to live by her own rules now.

She thumbed through her phone until she found her "upbeat" playlist and selected the song that Taylor had hated the most. The second the beat dropped, she let loose. Eyes closed, arms flailing, spinning like a drunk sailor on tilt-o-wheel kind of loose. She was free. And she was going to make the most of every second. Nothing had ever fel—

"Hi there."

Summer screamed, though the sound cut off halfway through as terror squeezed at her throat. She slapped a hand over her mouth, trying to hold back the hysterical laughter that was bubbling up so she didn't terrify the poor—and extremely hot, *hello*—young man who was standing there holding a box and giving her the most adorable sheepish grin she'd ever seen in her life.

"I'm sorry," he said, as she quickly punched at her phone to shut off the music. "I knocked but you must not have heard me over the..." He frowned. "What *was* that exactly?"

She gave him a sheepish grin of her own. "A group called *The SIDH*. It's sort of...techno bagpipe."

He nodded slowly like she was speaking a foreign language he was too polite to say he didn't understand. "Where did you come across something like that?"

"Late night Google search gone wrong."

He laughed, a deep, rich baritone of a rumble that made her toes curl in her favorite red and black plaid Tieks.

"It's an acquired taste," she said.

"Apparently." He chuckled again. "I'm sorry to just kind of barge in. Emily sent me over with..." He lifted the box Summer had hardly noticed. She was too busy noticing everything else.

Emily's texts suddenly made all the sense.

She hadn't just sent *someone*. She had sent quite possibly the hottest man Summer had ever seen in her life. She was pretty sure her lips pulled into a smile but whatever she'd intended to say came out in a breathy sort of squeak that didn't resemble any sound in the human language she could identify.

One of his dark eyebrows quirked up, his face radiating amusement. She needed to pull it together. Quickly.

"Sorry about...all that," she said, waving her hand around to encompass the full body twitch she'd been doing when he walked in. "I was just sort of having a solo going away dance party."

"Ah, is that what that was?"

Summer gave him a half grin. "Emily calls my dance style Muppet-flail-meets-meat-grinder."

He barked out another laugh. "Whatever it was, I dug it. I like a woman who knows how to move and isn't afraid to go for it."

His voice had dropped to that husky bedroom tone guys did when they were flirting (at least according to the movies she'd been watching lately—she'd never actually had a guy do it to her), and he seemed to be enjoying the leisurely voyage of her body his eyes were taking.

She'd normally be a little more self-conscious, but her eyes were doing a little wandering of their own. His dark hair was cropped close to his head in the classic military fade, and she really wanted to see more of the intriguing tattoo that was partially visible where his short sleeves ended. His soft black T-shirt molded to every inch of his chiseled-straight-from-stone chest. The poor sleeves looked incapable of containing themselves around his biceps. And with his tapered waist and hips hugged by low-slung jeans he was literally the definition of her very own wet dream come to life.

She was going to kill Emily for not giving her a head's up so she could have had some hope of preparing herself for what had to be at least six feet of delicious man candy. Even if he *was* too young for her to actually make a move. If she did things like make moves. Which she didn't.

He noticed her noticing him but instead of running screaming from the house, as she fully expected him to do, he bit his bottom lip. Her breath punched out of her lungs, and she had to dig her nails into her palm to keep her body from quivering in delight.

Just the thought of it had her doing a mental double take. She'd never quivered in her life. She'd never even used the word quiver. *No one* ever used that word in the real world. Yet there she was, on the edge of Quiver Town, with its mayor standing there grinning at her like he wasn't sure what she was going to do next, but he couldn't wait to find out.

Thank you, Emily.

Chapter 2

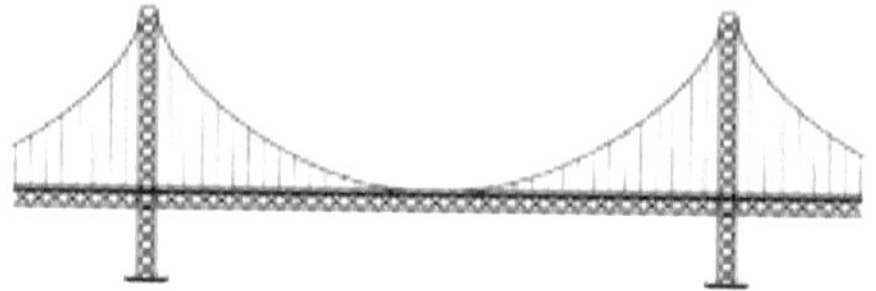

Summer took a deep breath and then counted slowly to ten in her mind, but neither of those centering techniques were working. Dropping to the floor for a full-on meditation moment would probably be a bit much. Though anything short of that was so not going to work in the face of such masculine sexiness.

Was there a mantra to keep your libido under control? What were the chances she could Google that without him noticing?

"I'm sorry, you never said, but you are Summer, aren't you?" he asked.

And there went her dubious control. A delightful little shiver skated up her spine at the sound of her name on his lips. His full, kissable, pouty lips.

She blinked and looked up into a pair of deep brown eyes and opened her mouth to answer...only no sound came out. He grinned again, apparently not finding it at all odd his mere presence had mentally incapacitated her. Probably happened to him all the time.

"Summer Laurent?" he asked again.

She gave her head a little shake. "Hi. Yes, sorry. You must be Emily's friend. She said she'd send someone with..." She pointed to the box in his hands, and he grinned again, lifting it a little.

"Yes. Well, more like an acquaintance really, by way of her sister. Sort of."

"Maggie?" Summer asked and the man nodded.

"I'm a friend of Maggie's husband. Liam and I go back a few years. I'm Garrett, by the way. Vogel."

"Hi," she said again, cringing when her cheeks grew warm. She was *not* blushing in front of this guy! She hadn't blushed since...well, never. She *never* blushed. "Thanks so much for bringing that over. I really appreciate it."

"No problem. I was over at Liam and Maggie's when Josh showed up. I guess Emily had left the box in his truck and she said she needed someone to bring this package over to you, so I volunteered."

"That was very kind of you."

"Actually, I should probably thank you. Josh brought their kids with him so they could play on the obstacle course so..."

He grinned a little sheepishly and Summer chuckled.

"I completely understand. I love them to death but for totally adorable little angels, they can be real devils sometimes."

He laughed and the sound reverberated through her chest.

"That's one way to put it. Anyway, when she offered the chance to escape—I mean to be of service—I jumped at it."

Summer chuckled again. "Well, I still really appreciate it, so thank you. You can just drop it anywhere."

"My pleasure," he said, bending over to put it beside the fireplace. He took his time straightening back up, his eyes roaming over her as he did.

That heated flash in his eyes was one she hadn't seen in a very long time. So long, she wasn't sure she'd actually seen it. Even when his eyes met hers again and their gazes locked. He gave her a slow, knowing smile that had her trying to suck a breath into her suddenly deficient lungs. It had been a very long time since a man had looked at her like that.

Or at least since she'd noticed.

Not that she was unattractive. When she dressed up, she could definitely pull some looks and wasn't half bad even if she didn't. But while Taylor had liked for her to be admired—as that reflected well on him—he didn't like for her to like it. So if looks had been coming her way, she had done her best to ignore them. But damn...she was looking now.

She squeezed her eyes shut for second, trying to get a hold of herself. What in the hell was going on? She had never gone so completely daft over someone before.

"This is a great house," he said, moving farther inside. "It must be hard to leave it."

She seized on the subject gratefully. The house she could discuss without swooning on the doorstep. Maybe. The master bath had a killer tub that made her knees weak.

"Yes and no. I just got divorced, so...out with the old, in with the new and all that."

She sounded like an idiot. She really had to get a grip.

"Well, I'm sorry about the divorce. But on the bright side, that means you're single." He waggled his eyebrows with a sexy little lip bite that had everything south of her navel perking up and paying attention.

Was she that hard up or was he just that hot?

Both?

Both.

A breathy little "Ha!" sound was about all she could manage as a response. The air felt much too thin in the room, but she swallowed and smiled back. "True. Too bad I'm way too old for you."

No way she'd just said that. Oh, holy hell, he must think...God, she didn't even know what he must be thinking. Probably mortified that some old chick was hitting on him. If he even recognized her weak attempt. She was a bit out of practice. He seemed like a pretty happy guy; he probably flirted with everybody. She really needed to make sure it didn't go to her head. Actually, if the house could fall on her head right now, that would be great.

He shrugged and looked her over again with an appraising look. "Age is just a number. And not a very interesting one."

She raised an eyebrow. "Spoken like someone who hasn't hit thirty yet."

He grinned. "True. But I'm definitely legal, so no worries."

She snorted. "If you're young enough to joke about being legal, you're too young."

"Naw, I'm twenty-six."

Oh God, yeah. Way too young. "Well, I'm thirty-four so that makes me way too—"

"Hot for me? I agree, but I promise I clean up nice."

The next sound that came out of her mouth was not one that resembled any other sound she'd ever made before in her life. It was probably a laugh. Possibly a sob. Who was this guy? And what was he doing to her? And could he keep doing it? Because she was getting all tingly just from a fairly normal convo, and she had really missed those tingles.

"So," he said, thankfully taking some pity on her and moving away to wander about the room. "How do you know Emily?"

Finally, some safe ground. "We've been best friends since college."

"She's a riot," he said with a half grin.

Summer grinned. "She's a little wacky, for sure, but I don't know what I'd do without her."

He nodded. "Good to have friends like that."

"It definitely is," she said with a smile. "How do you know Liam?"

"We served in the same unit before he left. We were deployed together a couple of times. He's a good guy. Saved my ass more than once. That dog of his though..."

Summer giggled and tried to cut the sound off when she realized how ridiculous it sounded. What was she doing? He wasn't being that funny, and she was laughing like she'd never heard anything so hilarious. Hormones just made everything entertaining apparently.

"Yeah, he's adorable but that's a whole lot of dog. I think he even makes my butt look small."

Garrett looked her over again, making a point of checking out her ass. She should probably be offended but...well, she did bring the topic up. And his face showed nothing but a total abject appreciation that sent a bolt of unfamiliar heat straight to her core. Damn. All that with one look?

"There's nothing wrong with some curves. I've always preferred them myself," he said, his voice somehow sounding lower, huskier. And *so* freaking sexy. Summer bit her lip to keep from making some really embarrassing sounds.

First year of college, she'd gained her freshman fifteen...times two. And the weight had stuck around even after they graduated. After she and Taylor had been married for a few years and things started to go downhill, she'd packed on a few more. She actually didn't totally hate it. Especially the magnificent rack that came along with a little extra weight. But Taylor seemed to want the classical trophy wife with the perfect body, perfect hair, perfect house, who smiled perfectly, acted perfectly, gave him perfect children. The perfect life.

Only his idea of perfect was a lot different than hers.

Still, she'd loved him. She'd thought. So, she'd given herself over to creating the perfect life for him even if it hadn't been what she really wanted. Everything except dropping the weight she couldn't seem to lose, even when she tried. Which admittedly wasn't often.

Or the children. She loved kids. But she'd never really wanted any of her own. She loved her career, really loved helping her speech therapy kids. And then she loved coming home to her clean, quiet house and decompressing. The fact that she'd never felt the urge to procreate had been one of the biggest issues between her and Taylor. Well, that and the fact that he just truly didn't seem to like her very much. Kind of an important part of a relationship, at least in her mind.

Garrett was still eyeing her curves like he wanted nothing more than to get his hands all over them, and if she were living in a fantasy land, she would absolutely be down for that. She'd drag him into the kitchen, hop up on the counter, and let him have his wicked, wicked way with her. She'd never thought of herself as cougar material—if being eight years older—okay, almost nine since her birthday was just a couple months away—constituted being a cougar—but then she'd never been faced with anyone so much younger who even remotely appealed to her. She typically went for older men. Taylor was six months older and was by far the youngest person she'd ever dated. And she'd definitely never been the one-night stand or momentary-fling-with-a-stranger type girl. But *dayum*. Garrett was about to change her religion.

"You hungry?" Garrett asked.

Summer blinked at him, trying to get her brain back on a functioning track. "Hungry?"

"Yeah. There's this great diner I always visit when I'm in the area. I'd love to take you."

"Oh...I..."

And that was about all she could get out before her brain short-circuited and started cascading through a million different scenarios. Most of which ended in some teenage waitress commenting on how cute it was that she took her little brother out for a burger (and if he could pass as her son, she would just drive off a cliff right then).

A car pulled into the driveway, giving her a slight reprieve before having to respond. Summer looked around Garrett's broad shoulders, trying to see out the still-open front door. She frowned. That couldn't be Taylor already, could it?

"Hold that thought," she said, hoping her smile didn't look as nervous as she felt. It had been a very long time since anyone had asked her on a date. And the last time someone Garrett's age had asked her, she'd been that age—well younger—herself.

"There's some beer and iced teas in the fridge if you want a drink," she said. "Since you did carry that heavy box all the way in here." She grinned. "I'll be right back. I'm going to go see who's here."

"Thanks," Garrett said. "A drink sounds great. And give that dinner a thought while you're gone." He winked at her as he walked past, and she got distracted admiring the view until the slam of the car door drew her attention back to the driveway.

Ugh. It *was* Taylor.

She hurried out of the house and down the porch steps. "Why are you here so early?" she asked. "You said you wouldn't be here until after six."

Taylor blinked in surprise, and she had to bite her tongue to keep from apologizing from questioning him. He was early. She had every right to say something and as they were no longer married, she didn't need to tiptoe around his temper anymore. Let him be irritated with her.

He finally shrugged, uncharacteristically unconcerned that he was disrupting their schedule and forcing his presence on her when she'd specifically asked him to keep his distance. The man lived for his schedules. Her deviating from a previously agreed upon schedule—or him thinking she had—had probably caused a good sixty percent of their arguments.

"I wanted to talk to you. Figured it would be best to do it in person, not over the phone."

She frowned. "Anything you have to say to me can be done by text. Or by email if your thumbs can't work that much. I can't imagine anything that would require us to have an actual conversation, let alone one face-to-face."

"Well, that just shows how much more consideration I have for you than you have for me."

Summer clenched her hands into fists, trying to will herself into her mental happy place.

Murder is wrong, murder is wrong...

Her gut still churned. The urge to say something to smooth things over was so strong she nearly shook with it. Taylor had never been physically abusive, but if things hadn't gone his way, he hadn't been shy in making his displeasure known. Sometimes it would start a fight. More often it would result in the silent treatment. Icy cold silence. For days. She would have rather he yelled. And he knew it.

So, she got really good at making sure his feathers were never ruffled. And it was a habit she really needed to break. This man had made her life hell for years and was fast on his way to making their divorce even worse. Though she had never been able to figure out if it was sheer cruelty on his part or if he really was just that clueless.

He sighed like her mere existence was a burden to him. "I know how dramatic you can get, and I didn't want you making a scene at the Bolnicast's wedding this weekend. The last thing you can afford to do is upset your headmaster, and more importantly, he's a very important client of mine. I need the contacts I get from him. And my news isn't really something you want to tell your ex-wife over a text."

She resisted the urge to roll her eyes. Barely. "What news?"

"My new girlfriend will be coming to the wedding with me. I hope you can be more civil to her than you were to the last one."

Summer glared. "Considering the fact that the last one was sitting in my breakfast nook, wearing my robe, and drinking coffee from my favorite mug when I met her, I think I was pretty civil."

And if she hadn't been, well shit, her uncivility had been, in her humble opinion, more than warranted.

Taylor's baffled face at that moment? Not so warranted.

"We were separated," he said, frowning at her like he couldn't figure out why she was so upset.

"I'd been gone less than twenty-four hours. I hadn't even taken a suitcase with me."

He shook his head, apparently thoroughly exasperated. "You asked for a divorce and walked out. You obviously didn't want me anymore, so I'm not quite sure why you cared if someone else did."

She closed her eyes and counted to ten. Then added a few more for good measure.

It might take more than a happy place to keep the homicide department from being called.

Chapter 3

The rumble of voices drifted to Garrett from the front porch, and he abandoned his iced tea on the counter and moved into the foyer.

He didn't really mean to eavesdrop but...ah, hell, who was he kidding? He absolutely meant to, or he wouldn't have tip-toed through the foyer like some cartoon villain until he was close enough to hear through the partially opened door. They'd just met, but he liked Summer. A lot. And what he could hear of her voice didn't sound happy.

Josh had asked him to bring the box over for Emily, and he hadn't minded doing a favor for his best friend's sister-in-law's husband, especially since it got him out of the way of their offspring. Not that he didn't love kids. He did. He'd always wanted a big family himself eventually. But Josh and Emily's kids were...a lot. So, the chance to make a break for it had been welcome. Had he known what would be waiting for him, he would have jumped in his truck with bells on. Or tassels, maybe. Summer was an unexpected surprise. A very welcome, unexpected surprise.

The fact that she was eight years older than him didn't matter a bit. Twenty or forty, the woman had curves for days and thick curly brown hair that he wanted to dig his fingers into. Not to mention those hazelnut eyes with the tiniest flakes of green that he could spend all day staring into. She also amused him which he frankly needed in his life. She was a damn dream come true, is what she was. Gorgeous, funny, soft and sweet, with a laugh that he wanted to record so he could listen to it anytime he felt down. And that was how he felt after fifteen minutes. He wanted to spend the next fifteen hours in her company. Fifteen days. Possibly weeks. Maybe even longer.

He didn't know who the hell her ex was, but the man was certifiably stupid for letting her go. Garrett had only known her minutes and could tell how special she was. A man who couldn't figure that out in several years didn't deserve her.

He walked closer to the open door, trying to hear what they were saying. There was a distinct rumble of a man's voice talking, and Summer didn't sound happy when she answered.

"Regardless of our past differences, this wedding is an important event for our social circle. And it's not like you can back out anyway. He's your boss. You can't afford to lose this job now that I'm not footing your bills."

"Nice," she said, her voice dripping with disgust.

"What? Is that incorrect?"

She sighed. "No. It's not incorrect."

Garrett snorted, mentally filling in the part she left out. *Not wrong, but still a dick move to point it out.*

"Look, you weren't real thrilled running into my last girlfriend without a heads up—"

"Again, we'd been split up for less than a day, Taylor. And she was *in my house.*"

"So, I just wanted you to be prepared this time, that's all," the guy said, completely ignoring her comment.

"You dating is not the end of my world, Taylor. It's not even a novel experience for me. Hell, you were probably dating the whole time we were married."

Garrett could hear the guy's—Taylor's?—obnoxious sigh from where he stood inside the house. He'd never wanted to hit a man he'd never met so much in his life.

"See, it was this kind of reaction I wanted to avoid this weekend. You always have to be so dramatic over the tiniest things."

Oh hell. Those were fighting words right there.

Maybe he should go out and hold her earrings. Or better yet, hold Taylor down for her...

"First of all, sometimes a little drama is justified..."

Garrett nodded. *Damn straight, baby, you tell him.*

"But apparently our definitions of drama differ completely because I am *not* being dramatic," she continued. "Even if I was, I would never do anything to ruin my boss's, or *anyone's*, wedding, no matter how big of an ass you were being. And secondly, my reaction isn't because you're bringing a date. It's because you decided to encroach upon my private time to try and rub it in after we agreed we'd stay out of each other's way."

Taylor released a long-suffering sigh that had Garrett seeing red and he didn't even know the guy. "Since you never had any trouble going against whatever schedules or agreements we'd made in the past, I really didn't think you'd mind now."

Garrett could feel her outraged gasp down to his toes.

"That is a lie, and you know it. I always made the utmost effort to stick to your schedules, but that's completely beside the point. I'm glad you have a date. Good for you. I assumed you *would* have one. You aren't the type of guy who can handle being alone. Not really sure why you think I care or why you felt the need to tell me in person."

Taylor snorted. "I'm fine being alone. I've just never had to be."

His tone implied the *unlike some people* so clearly, he might as well have just said it. Garrett gritted his teeth. Oh, this guy was really doubling down on the assholery.

"I was trying to be nice," he said. "No one wants to get bad news by text."

"It's not bad news, Taylor. It's barely news at all."

He ignored her again, rambling on as though she'd never spoken. "Since I had to come here anyway, I figured kill two birds and all that."

"Fine. Good. Whatever. You delivered your message. Congrats. If you'll excuse me—"

"Also," Taylor said, and Summer sighed. "Since I know how women are about these things, you should probably know that she's quite a bit younger than you and a model. You may have heard of her. Carolina Burchek? She was on that model reality show a few seasons ago."

"You know nothing about how women are, Taylor. I couldn't care less who she is or what her statistics are. And sorry. Not a show I've ever watched."

"Well, she's got a pretty big following so she might have some fans among the guests this weekend which I thought might make things more difficult for you. I know how self-conscious you always get around women who are...well..."

Garrett couldn't see his face but his condescendingly "caring" tone and the slight pause after those words painted the picture all too well. He was making a comparison, and, in his eyes, it wasn't favoring Summer.

"If you value your balls, you won't finish that sentence."

Ha! Tell him, Summer.

"See, this is what I was talking about. I'm just trying to be civil here. I didn't want you to be blindsided in front of all our friends. I know you don't have a date—"

"How would you know whether or not I have a date?"

"Because I talked to Tony last week, and he said Janine said you hadn't RSVP'd for a plus one."

"You called them instead of just asking me? Are you in middle school or something?"

"Like I said, I was trying to avoid some big scene—"

"You aren't trying to avoid it. You purposely came here when you knew I'd be here to *create* one."

She wasn't wrong. Dumbass couldn't argue that point.

"Only so it wouldn't happen in front of everyone else."

Right. Garrett rolled his eyes.

"This'll be the first function that we are attending as divorced couple," Taylor said. "And I jus—"

"We aren't attending as a divorced couple. We aren't a couple in any way anymore. Just two people who happen to be divorced who will be in the same vicinity for a few hours."

"Whatever. You know what I mean. I guess this is what I get for trying to be nice."

Summer snorted. "This is you being nice? I don't think that word means what you think it means."

Garrett quietly chuckled. He'd never actually seen that old *Princess Bride* movie, but he'd seen enough memes to get the reference. Excellent burn.

"Quit being so juvenile, Summer. I figured the whole situation would be awkward for you. Since you can't back out, I just wanted you to know ahead of time so you wouldn't be embarrassed when I walk in with a gorgeous model and you're standing there alone."

That was it. Garrett didn't need to know anything else about the man. His gloating self-centered digs made Garrett wish he could send the man packing—with his teeth in his glove box. But he couldn't really kick him off his own property. He could, however, give him a little taste of his own medicine. And then some.

Before he could go outside though, he caught a glimpse of Summer turning and heading up the steps into the house.

"Shit," Garrett muttered, turning to hurry across the foyer and out of sight before they made it inside.

Perfect. Nothing says 'hey, I'm a great date prospect, give me a shot' like getting caught eavesdropping.

Chapter 4

Garrett darted into the kitchen just as the door opened and their footsteps echoed across the foyer's marble tiles. He grabbed his iced tea and leaned against the counter like he hadn't nearly been caught spying on them.

"Embarrassed?" Summer said, as they turned the corner into the kitchen. "The only thing I'm embarrassed about is that we were ever together. What the fu—"

"Who the hell are you?" Taylor said, glaring at Garrett.

Before he could answer, Summer sashayed up to him and kissed him full on the lips. "Sorry for keeping you waiting, babe. Had an unexpected visitor."

Garrett, lips still tingling, tried to reboot his brain so he could respond. Easier said than done since all his body wanted to do was plaster itself to Summer and let her do that again. A few dozen times.

Summer froze, her eyes pleading with him. It wasn't exactly what he'd had in mind, but he was so down with any plan that included kissing those luscious lips of hers.

He wrapped his arm around her shoulders and pulled her against him, kissing her temple. "You're always worth the wait, baby. Is this guy bothering you?" he said, nodding in Taylor's direction without bothering to look at him while he smoothed his thumb across Summer's cheek.

The thousand-watt smile she aimed at him took his breath away. Good God, she was breathtaking.

She stretched up on her toes to plant another warm, sweet kiss on his lips that was over far too soon. He was tempted to try for a third when she glanced at the asshat who was now sporting a mottled red face. "Yeah, he is. But he's my ex, so I think that's in the job description. Don't worry about him. He's harmless."

The asshat in question turned his glare on Summer. "Who the hell is this?"

Ah, the sweet smell of a bully getting his panties in a bunch first thing in the morning. Nothing like it.

Garrett grinned and did the universal guy head nod in Taylor's direction. "Garrett Vogel. Summer's boyfriend."

Summer tensed in his arms but didn't refute his claim. And the look of absolute shock on the asshat's face made the whole thing worth it.

Garrett took advantage of Taylor's sputtering to rub it in a little more. "Are you like a door-to-door salesman or something? We're not interested, if you are. Unless you're selling some of that pink cleanser stuff. That stuff is seriously amazing," he said, turning to Summer. "We could definitely use that in—"

"I'm the owner of this house," Taylor nearly spat out in what he probably thought was a menacing tone. It was almost adorable. Look at that, he was puffing out his chest and everything. Garrett almost wanted to take a picture for the fridge.

"Half-owner," Summer pointed out. Her ex shot her a nasty look, but she ignored him. "Garrett, this is Taylor."

The guy looked at him like Garrett should start shaking in his combat boots. Garrett knew exactly who the guy was. But the fact that Taylor wanted and expected him to know who he was made Garrett even more determined to push his buttons.

He put on his best blank look and just waited for Taylor to keep explaining.

He didn't disappoint. Taylor's eyes widened and he clenched his jaw so hard Garrett swore he heard it pop. "Taylor Laurent."

"Laurent?" Garrett asked, pasting on his blandest, most polite-to-hide-that-I'm-bored smile. "An old relative of yours?" he asked Summer.

She sucked both lips in and bit down, obviously trying not to laugh. Taylor frowned, looking pissed and confused that he wasn't getting the rise out of Garrett he wanted.

"Her husband," he said.

Garrett raised his eyebrow and Summer said, "Ex-husband."

"Ah!" Garrett said. "When you said owner, I thought maybe you were the one buying the place. My bad. I forgot that Summer had been married before. Don't think she ever mentioned your name. Sorry about that."

Taylor scowled, his chest puffing out again with the air he dragged in through his nose. Riling this guy up was too damn fun.

Taylor looked Garrett up and down, and Garrett had to bite his lip to keep from laughing at the look on Taylor's face. The guy was obviously pissed as hell that Garrett was there. But he was equally obviously intimidated by the sheer size of Garrett. Garrett wasn't the tallest guy in a crowd by any means. He hit six feet, but just barely. Even so, he still had a good three or so inches on Taylor. And a great deal more inches when it came to muscle. And judging by the guy's attitude, Garrett was probably packing a few extra inches a little further south of the border, too.

"So, what do you do, Gary?" Taylor asked with the most pretentious look Garrett had ever seen on someone who was not some sort of distant royal or hundred-year-old socialite.

"I'm a bomb diffuser," Garrett deadpanned, his best poker face in place. He didn't bother to correct Taylor's use of the wrong name. The guy was obviously doing it to get under his skin, and Garrett had no intention of giving him the satisfaction. Though that didn't mean he wouldn't join in the game. "What do you do, Tracy? Aside from owning this house that is."

Summer had started wheezing faintly through her nose, and Garrett wasn't sure if it was from trying to hold back laughter or something else, but he was too afraid to look at her to find out. One look at her trying not to contain the mirth and he wouldn't be able to hold it in either.

"The name is Taylor," he bit out. He obviously wasn't as good at dealing with jackasses as Garrett was. "And I work in the finance industry." His derisive gaze looked Garrett up and down again and then he waved his hand dismissively. "My actual job description is probably too complicated and boring for someone...in your line of work. What was it you said you did again?"

Right. Like he'd forgotten already.

"I'm a hostage negotiator."

Summer turned the squeak that erupted from her into a cough. Taylor's irritated glance flashed to her before landing back on Garrett's most angelically innocent face.

"I thought you said you were a bomb diffuser."

Garrett shrugged. "If you already knew, why did you ask?"

Taylor's eyes narrowed, and Garrett raised his brows a fraction. *Your move, moron.*

Taylor apparently decided pushing the point wasn't going to work out in his favor because he let it go and nodded in the direction of Garrett's head.

"You in the military?" Taylor asked, staring at Garrett's close-cropped brown hair with a wrinkled nose.

Jackass.

Summer tightened her grip on his waist like she was afraid he might be getting tired of Taylor's nonsense. He pressed another kiss to her temple and drew her in closer. Not because he needed her to hold him back. He'd dealt with worse assholes than Taylor Laurent. Naw. He just really enjoyed having her pressed up against him. And not just because Taylor's blood pressure visibly increased every time she touched him.

"Yes, sir," Garrett said, answering with a pride that he doubted Taylor had ever felt a day in his life. "Army."

Taylor smirked. "You don't need to call me sir. I'm not your superior...at least rank-wise." He chuckled with a smug look that would have tempted a man less used to controlling his impulses to knock off.

Instead, Garrett leveled his best smile at Taylor and laid on the charm. "Oh, I know that. It's just that my mama always taught me to respect my elders, and I always try to do my mama proud."

Summer choked off another laugh and pressed her face into his chest though her shoulders kept shaking.

Taylor openly eyed the two of them with contempt though he tried to keep up the fake polite routine. "And what does your mama think of..." He waved a finger at them, like he couldn't quite spit out the words.

Garrett smiled bigger. "She's thrilled. If I'm happy, my mom's happy. And I've never been happier," he said, looking down at Summer who actually blushed. She was so friggin' cute.

"I'm surprised she's not concerned that Summer is so much older than you," Taylor said to Summer.

She frowned and spoke before Garrett could say anything. "You're one to talk. How do what's-her-face's parents feel about you? And what does my age have to do with anything?"

Taylor plastered a fake concerned look on his face. "Oh, I'm sorry. Was he not aware of how old you are?" He turned to Garrett like they were buddies. "I know women tend to want to keep that little number to themselves the older they get. And she's pushing forty now so—"

"I'm thirty-four, Taylor. That's hardly pushing forty."

What was this guy's deal? He was acting like Summer was in her 50's, not 30's. And even if she *was* in her 50's, she'd have rocked circles around most of the other women he'd dated lately. Who gave a flying fuck how old she was?

"It was one of the first things she told me. Though honestly, I couldn't care less. Age is the last thing I look for in a woman."

"Unlike some people," she said, her tone heavily implying that's exactly what Taylor did.

He shrugged. "I guess age doesn't mean much as long as the couple have something in common. Carolina and I met at the gym. It's really wonderful finally spending time with someone who shares my interests, you know? Well, I mean, you obviously *don't*, but then they do say opposites attract. I guess." His gaze flicked between the two of them and lingered on Summer's luscious curves with a look that was obviously meant to be insulting.

The sharp intake of breath from Summer was the only indication she gave that Taylor's insult had hit home. Garrett tightened his arm around her, and she looked up at him, pain and anger flashing through her eyes. Okay, they were going to have to get out of here soon or he was going to introduce Taylor's face to the pavement.

He held her tighter, rubbing his hand up and down her arm. "I don't know about opposites, but I definitely get the attraction part," he said, giving her a heated look that had her biting that luscious bottom lip again before he tore his eyes from her to glance back at Taylor.

Taylor looked confused, and for the hundredth time in less than five minutes, Garrett wondered what Summer had seen in this guy.

"Don't bother trying to explain it to him," she said, wrapping her other arm around Garrett's waist so she was hugging him from the side. "As long as you get it, I'm good."

He gazed down at her, drinking in those deep brown eyes of hers. "Oh, you're more than good," he said, tracing her full bottom lip with his thumb, soothing the faint mark left by her teeth. "And I definitely get it."

"Do you?" she murmured breathlessly, tilting her face up a fraction more so it was at the perfect angle if he leaned down. Just a bit.

"Oh yeah," he said, the words coming out as more of a growl. All he had to do was close those last few inches between them and—

"Hello?" Taylor said, his voice raised enough that Garrett suspected it wasn't the first time he had said it.

"What?" he asked, dragging out the word even though he knew full well it made him sound like a pouty teenager. Summer laughed, and he grinned at her. Okay, so he was totally acting like a pouty teenager, but damn it, he'd been *this close* to kissing her again.

Taylor scowled. "I said I guess I'll see you two at the wedding."

"Wedding?" Garrett asked. Then mentally kicked himself when Summer stiffened in his arms.

Taylor raised his eyebrows in delighted surprise. "Oh. Sorry. I figured with you being her boyfriend and all she would have invited you to her boss's wedding."

"I just haven't had a chance to discuss it with him yet—" Summer said, but Taylor cut her off.

"The wedding is this weekend, and you've known about it for months." He furrowed his forehead like he was confused but it was all too obvious he was enjoying catching her in the lie. "I mean, I get it. You've never been really big on going out anyway and you hate being the center of attention. Probably why you haven't told anyone about your..." He jerked his head over toward Garrett. "What do they call you guys nowadays? Sugar babies? Cougar cubs?"

He smirked, and Garrett had to grit his teeth to keep from telling the guy off. Not that he was worried about upsetting the dickwad. But there was no way in hell he'd give Taylor the satisfaction of getting a rise out of him.

"Oh, grow up, Taylor," Summer said, sounding just as fed up with her ex as Garrett. Though both she and Taylor looked surprised at her outburst.

Taylor held up his hands. "Hey, I get it if you're too embarrassed to be seen together."

"Seriously?" Summer let go of Garrett and took a step toward Taylor, her hands fisted at her sides. "*No one* would be embarrassed to be seen with him, least of all me."

"I was thinking more of him. I know how my friends would have acted when I was his age if I'd been dating someone like you."

"What's that's supposed to mean?"

"I'm just saying—"

"You're acting like we're some sort of circus side show. Hell, there's less of an age difference between me and Garrett than between you and Angina...Vagina...whatever her name is."

"You are very well aware her name is Carolina," Taylor said, his fake polite façade completely gone. "And she may be younger than me, but she's very mature for her age, and like it or not people are just more accepting of a guy dating someone a bit younger than they are of a middle-aged woman dragging around some rented boy toy unless you're some Hollywood A-lister or something, and you are definitely n—"

"Excuse me?" The fact that her voice was kind of quiet and even-toned somehow made it sound more dangerous. Garrett wouldn't want that tone aimed at him.

Though at this point, he wasn't sure either of them even remembered he was standing there. Maybe things were getting a little too heated. Not that he wouldn't enjoy watching Summer knock her ex down a peg or two, because he absolutely deserved it. But he didn't want her to do or say anything she'd regret later, either. Though that didn't mean he was going to let Taylor get away with his gross disrespect and attempts to hurt Summer.

Summer glared at Taylor. "Garrett is *not* my boy toy."

Time to break things up a bit. Though he kind of liked Summer defending his honor.

"Naw," Garrett said, grinning but in as non-threatening of a manner as possible. "I think the new term is tender vittles. Because they eat us up. And good *God*, the eatin' is good," he said, letting his voice go pre-orgasmically growly.

Summer looked up at him with wide, shocked eyes, and he winked at her before looking back over at Taylor. "But Summer isn't nearly old enough to qualify for a cougar. Though I'd still be beggin' at this goddess's feet even if she was. Besides, I prefer stud muffin if you really want to put a label on it."

Taylor snorted. "Stud muffin?"

"Oh yeah," Garrett said, taking Summer's hand and pulling her back into his arms so he could stare down into her eyes. "Because muffins are delicious and good for you and...well," he said, waving his hand toward his body like he was Vanna White showcasing the prize behind Door Number Three. "I *am* a stud."

Taylor sputtered, but Garrett didn't give him time to respond. "As for being embarrassed to be seen together, you're out of your mind. She certainly has no reason to be embarrassed for living her life how she sees fit. And I've never been prouder of the woman at my side. The only problem we have," he said, drawing her in even closer so that she was plastered to him, "is that's she's so damn sexy, I can't seem to keep my hands off her."

She wrapped her arms around his waist and nestled against him even more, some of the tension draining from her as she did. Yeah, time to get away from this guy. They'd made their point, and there was no reason to keep giving the ass their time or energy.

He snuggled into Summer, groaning low in his throat and putting a little extra oomph into it for Taylor's benefit. "Damn baby, I gotta get you home."

He swept her up into his arms, grinning at her surprised giggle, and took a couple steps toward the door before turning back.

"Oh, and the whole wedding misunderstanding is my fault," he said to Taylor. "I just got back in town, unexpectedly early, so Summer probably wasn't sure if I'd be able to make it. But since I'm here, I'll absolutely be there with her. See you there. Now, if you'll excuse us, we've got a little catching up to do."

He nodded at Taylor and headed back out the door. Summer grabbed her purse from the hook by the door without him breaking his stride, and he didn't stop until they got to his truck.

The second they were both inside she turned to him. "Oh my God, I can't believe that just happened. You were amazing. Thank you so much. I'm so sorry you got sucked into all this. You don't really have to go to the wedding with me. I can make some excuse. Despite what Taylor says, I'm not *that* pathetic. I'll survive seeing him with whatever her name is. I just—"

Garrett grinned and started the truck but leaned closer to her before taking it out of gear. "First of all, you have absolutely no need to apologize. That guy is a total ass."

She snorted. "No argument here."

"And second of all, I meant what I said. I like you. You're funny, sassy, and hot as hell. I'd be thrilled to be your date for the wedding. And any other time. Rubbing your ex's nose in it is just an entertaining perk."

She stared at him, sort of stunned. "I don't know..."

"Oh, come on. Even if you're not interested in me and...forgive the conceit but I think you are, at least a little..." he said, drawing a finger down her cheek and smiling when a tremulous little sign escaped her lips.

"Maybe," she said, her voice barely audible.

"Um hm." He straightened and gripped the wheel again. "Either way, there is no way I'm letting you show up alone after all that," he said with a nod toward the house.

She still hesitated a second but then slowly nodded. "Okay. In that case, the wedding is on Saturday at four."

"I'll be there."

Her face clouded and she frowned. "Shit. Actually, it's kind of a destination thing. Not that far from here, but it's one of those whole weekend things. I can't ask—"

"I'm in," Garrett said, not pausing to think about it.

He was definitely getting himself in much deeper than he'd anticipated, but there was no way he was giving that asshole the satisfaction of seeing Summer alone. Besides, spending the whole weekend with Summer? Hell *yes*.

He pulled the truck out of the driveway and looked back over at her. "Where to?"

She pulled out her phone and fired off a text. "Let me see where Emily is. I've got a few things to say to her."

He grinned, and Summer's lips pulled into an answering smile though she wouldn't hold his gaze but stared at her phone.

"She's still at Liam's place," she said.

"Perfect. I was heading there anyway. What about your car?" he said, nodding to her Jeep Cherokee still sitting in the driveway. Though it was now blocked by Taylor's car.

"I'll come back and get it later. I really don't feel like dealing with him again just to get him to move it."

"As you wish," he said with a wink. Pulling out another one of those lines that were constantly making the meme rounds was a bit cheesy, sure, but it made her smile, and he was all about that.

Now he just needed to convince her to date him for real.

He loved a challenge.

Chapter 5

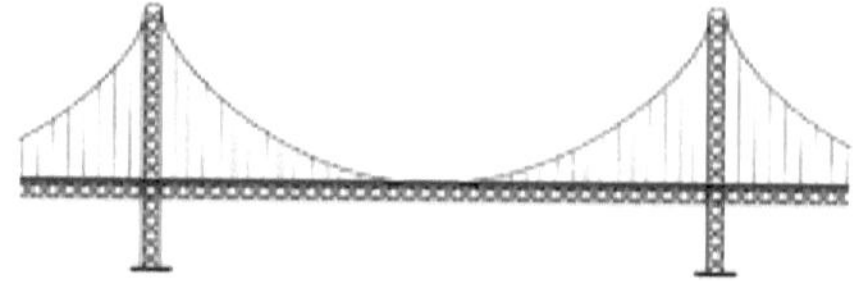

They pulled up to the building that Liam and Maggie owned, and Summer hopped out of the truck, wanting to get to Emily before Garrett did. Maggie was Emily's sister, but Summer had been friends with them all so long, she was sort of an unofficial third sister. Liam treated her as another sister-in-law, and they all spent most of their free time hanging out together.

The newly paved parking lot only held a few cars...Liam's and Josh's trucks, Maggie's Tesla, and Emily's minivan. Usually, the place was hopping with customers there for the amazing American Ninja courses. The adult-sized courses were great for those training for the actual show or for those who just wanted to be jacked enough in theory. And the kiddie courses were guaranteed to make your kids sleep a full ten-hour night by the time they were done. It was a popular place. Liam and Maggie were just finishing some bi-annual renovations though, so the place was momentarily empty except for the family.

Summer pushed open the door and looked around. The sound of children playing filtered in from the open door in the back that led to the outdoor course, so Emily's children were most likely there. Which meant that Emily was probably hiding out somewhere enjoying some kid-free time. And there was only one really comfortable place to hide out in this joint.

Summer marched straight to Liam's office and pushed open the door without knocking.

"You should have picked a better hiding spot," she said to her friend who looked up from one of the dozens of romance novels Liam kept stocked in the office. His "not so guilty pleasure" he liked to call them.

Because pleasure shouldn't make you feel guilty. A reading habit he'd picked up from a friend of his that owned a paintball course and gun range on the other side of town. He had a point and one that was pretty apt for her current situation, but she didn't want to acknowledge that just yet. She wanted to yell at Emily for getting her into this mess.

Emily shrugged. "Eh, you love me too much to hurt me."

"That's debatable," Summer said, though she couldn't keep the smile from her lips.

"Sooo.....did you enjoy that surprise I sent you?" she asked and then laughed before Summer could answer.

Summer sighed and shut the door, then advanced on her friend. "A heads-up would have been nice. Or not sending him at all. Why did you send him?"

Emily shrugged. "I really did forget the box, and when I remembered he was just sitting here...all hunked up and gorgeous...and you were over there in that big empty house all alone... What can I say? I saw a need, and I figured I'd help fill it. Or send someone to fill it for me." She waggled her eyebrows. "Please tell me you were smart and took advantage of the situation for once in your life."

Summer narrowed her eyes. "That situation has a name. And is almost ten years younger than me! What were you thinking?"

"Um, I was thinking he was probably getting tired of hanging out being a third wheel with Liam and Maggie and he looked like he could use a little entertainment. He's bored and horny, and you're alone and horny. I figured you guys could help each other out."

"Seriously?"

"What? Oh, come on, you can't tell me he isn't your walking wet dream. I can see you contemplating it right now."

Summer folded her arms. "Am not."

Emily snorted. "You're not fooling me no matter what you're telling yourself."

Summer narrowed her eyes. She wasn't going to admit anything, and Emily knew it...at least going by the groan her bestie let loose.

"Come on, girl. Do yourself a little favor. And by do yourself, I mean do him."

Summer's jaw dropped. "Holy shit, Em!"

Emily raised an eyebrow. "You keep screeching like you weren't drooling over him the second he walked in, and I'm going to go buy you a set of pearls to clutch while you're doing it. Fess up. He's the best present I ever got you."

Hell yeah, he was. "He's a person, not a present."

"He's a *hot* person who also happens to have an amazing personality to match. He is the total, complete package. Sweet, funny, willing and available, and probably able to make you come just from winking at you across the room."

"Emily!" One more jaw-drop and Summer's jaw was going to lock.

"Summer!" her BFF said, mimicking Summer's shocked tone.

She narrowed her eyes. "You're horrible."

Emily just grinned. "This is true. But you love me anyway. So, tell me everything."

Summer snorted and dropped into the chair on the other side of Liam's desk. "There's nothing to tell."

"Are you sure about that?" Emily asked grabbing her phone and scrolling through something. "Because according to Janine who heard from Tony who heard from an apparently very pissed off Taylor, you got yourself a new little boy toy that you're bringing to their wedding."

"Wow. News travels fast."

Emily leaned across the desk. "So, something did happen! Come on! The most unexpectedly exciting thing to happen to me in the last month was when I tripped over a Lego and Josh accidentally caught me by the boob. Let me live vicariously through you. Spill it!"

Summer sighed. "He's not my boy toy. That is such a ridiculously insulting term. He apparently prefers the term tender vittle. Or stud muffin," she said, unable to keep from smiling.

"He actually said that?"

"Yes."

"To Taylor?"

"Yes."

Emily's laughter pealed out and she nearly bounced in her chair. "Oh man, I would have paid very good money to have seen that."

Summer's lips twitched again. "Yeah. It was kind of awesome."

"No shit," Emily said, her face lit with amusement. Then her forehead crinkled. "Wait, if nothing happened, as you say, then why does Taylor think Garrett's coming with you to the wedding this weekend?"

Summer rubbed her hands over her face and then folded her arms on the desk and dropped her head onto them. Face down. "Because he is."

"Ha! I knew it!"

Summer looked up at her. "He's only doing it out of pity."

"I doubt that."

Summer shook her head. "No, really. Taylor showed up acting like a dick as usual and Garrett overheard him and acted like he was my boyfriend just to get Taylor off my back. But then one thing led to another, and he kind of got roped into going to the wedding."

Emily looked skeptical. "I've known Garrett a while. No one ropes him into anything. If he didn't want to go, he wouldn't be going. Besides, I heard it was a bit more than just him saying he was going to the wedding. Janine said Tony said Taylor said Garrett couldn't keep his hands off you."

Summer dropped her head back into her hands. "You have got to be kidding me. It's like middle school all over again. Except you guys are gossiping with my *boss*. I have to work with this guy you know."

Emily snorted. "Eh, Tony is more of a friend than a boss. And he'd be the first one to find this situation hilarious. He's always been more Team Summer. Taylor just gives him stock tips. You are the best speech therapist his school has ever had."

"Maybe. The rest of my comment still stands."

She chuckled. "Sorta. Except unlike middle school, the guys are actually hot, and you can actually do something with them."

Summer put a little extra outrage in her gasp and threw a pad of Post-its at her.

Emily dodged it and gave Summer her best angelic look. "What? I'm just saying the guy is seriously hot and you are seriously insane if you don't take advantage of that shit."

Summer frowned. "I'm not going to take advantage of him. Especially when he's just trying to be nice and get me out of the crappy situation."

"Oh please. The man doesn't even know you but was all over you while stepping up to defend you from your asshole ex. And you know damn well you enjoyed it, or you wouldn't be acting all guilty right now. Which makes me think more happened than you are admitting. Which makes me even *more* sure that he'd be more than down to do...whatever," she said looking Summer up and down with a mischievous glint in her eyes.

"Emily!" She was beginning to sound like a broken record.

Her innocent look was back. "What?" Along with the mocking tone.

"Even if I thought, *maybe*, that he would be fun to date..."

"Ha!" Emily said, opening her mouth to say more. But Summer held her finger up to stop her.

"Even if all of that was true, he is still way too young for me."

Emily rolled her eyes. "Whatever. A, he's not that much younger, and B, even if he was, who cares? From what I've heard, Taylor's new girlfriend is barely out of high school, and nobody bats an eyelash at that. So why the hell shouldn't you get in on some of that action? Especially when that action is smoking hot and looking to get itself in on you?"

Summer opened her mouth, but Emily beat her to it. "Yeah, I know. Emily!" She rolled her eyes again, and Summer couldn't help but smile again.

Emily smirked at her. "You know I'm right."

"You are so *not*."

Emily just shrugged and gave Summer that smug, confident smile again. "Pretty sure I am."

Summer rubbed her hands over her face again and groaned.

Emily threw her hands up. "Why are you fighting it so hard?"

"Because it's...messy! I don't even know the guy. He's too young. He's...he's...military."

"Yeah, which means he's in great shape and hot in his uniform. I'm not seeing the problem."

Summer raised an eyebrow. "It also means he could leave at any moment for any length of time which means there's no stability there. Not to mention I'd never know if he was coming back. I don't know how military families do it."

"He's almost at the end of his contract, and I don't think he was reupping, according to Liam anyway. So that might not be as much of an issue as you think."

"There's still just too many...unknown variables."

Emily rolled her eyes. "Yeah. That's kind of the point of dating. To get to know someone. Make all those unknowns known. It doesn't just happen like some sort of spontaneous combustion."

Summer sighed. "I know. But I'm not sure I'm ready to start dating again even if there weren't any other possible issues. Dating is such a crapshoot. I'm just getting my life pulled back together. I don't need to throw a wrench into things now."

"You've been saying the same thing for months." She held up a hand. "If you're truly not ready, then fine. But I know you too well, Summer. I think you're more than ready. You're just scared."

She wasn't wrong. And Summer *had* been itching for something more lately. Something outside the safe little cocoon she'd built around herself after she'd left Taylor. She was ready for something more. Probably. But...

Emily released an exasperated sigh that had Summer's lips twitching. "Stop thinking so hard. Come on, the guy is perfect for you. And before you protest again, I'm not saying marry the guy. I'm not even saying exclusively date him. But you haven't gone out at all since Taylor, and you abandoned that sinking ship a year ago. Time to get back in the saddle; go ride a cowboy."

Summer snorted. "I don't think that's how that saying goes."

"Eh," Emily said with a shrug. "That's the meaning if not the actual words. My point stands. You need to have some fun. Dip a toe back in the dating pool. So why not do it with a hot young stud who is ready and willing to get your engine going and has the most potential to piss off Taylor at the same time?"

The look on Taylor's face when Garrett had pulled her into his arms *had* been seriously priceless. "Yeah. That *was* kind of fun. You should've been there."

Emily clapped her hands. "Tell me everything!"

Summer grinned. "I would, but that would just be rewarding your bad behavior."

"Oh, come on," Emily said, but Summer ignored her.

"Besides, I left him sitting in the truck, so I should probably go—"

"Wait," Emily said, interrupting her. "He's here?" She jumped up from the desk.

Summer followed suit. "Emily...sit down. You are *not* going to—Em!"

But Emily had bolted from the room before Summer could finish getting her whole name out.

"Ah shit!" Summer hurried after her.

She needed to catch up before that little tornado got to Garrett and blew up something else in her life.

Chapter 6

Garrett had watched Summer's fine ass sashay into the building with utter delight before he jumped out of the truck to follow her. Damn, but he loved watching that woman walk away.

Liam's voice filtered around from the back of the building so Garrett headed back that direction instead of following Summer. She seemed like she could use a minute.

"Hey," Liam said when he saw Garrett walking up. "How'd the delivery go?"

Liam gave him a crooked grin and Garrett shook his head with a laugh. "You knew what Emily was up to, didn't you?"

Liam held up his hands. "You can't blame Emily's shenanigans on me. We aren't even blood related."

"Oh great." Maggie, Liam's wife and Emily's sister, finished wiping her hands off on a towel and put down the paintbrush she held to wander over to them. "What did my sister do now?"

Liam grinned and jerked a thumb at Garrett. "She sent him over to Summer's with that box of Taylor's crap."

Maggie's eyebrows hit her hairline. "That meddlesome little pain in the ass."

Garrett folded his arms and looked between the two of them. "You know if you guys wanted to set this up, all you had to do with ask."

Maggie held her hands up in an excellent imitation of her husband and shook her head. "Don't look at us. Emily is her own boss."

"I mean, I'm not complaining," Garrett said. "In fact, I'm a little pissed you guys didn't think to set this up before."

Liam raised an eyebrow. "Really?"

"Hell yeah. The woman is fine, funny, and free to date. The perfect F trifecta. I can't believe you had a single friend that hot and didn't think I might like to meet her."

Liam shrugged. "I honestly didn't think she'd be your type. You guys are kind of looking for the exact opposite things in life, plus she's a bit..." He paused, his gaze flicking to Maggie. "Older."

Maggie rolled her eyes.

Garrett snorted and waved that away. "It's not like she's thirty years older than me and looking for someone to sweep her off her walker. And even if she was, I wouldn't care."

"Well, she did also just get out of a marriage," Maggie added.

"Oh yeah. *That* piece of work."

Liam raised an eyebrow again. "Taylor showed up while you were there?"

"Ugh. The Cockroach," Maggie said. "I'm sorry that she's having to go through all of this, but I'm not sorry to see him go."

"Yeah," Garrett said. "I could only take about two and a half minutes of listening to his shit before I had to insert myself in the situation."

Liam opened his mouth to say something else, but before he could, the back door crashed open, and they all turned just as Emily slid to an abrupt halt in the yard. Summer, hot on her heels, nearly crashed into her.

"Well, hello there," Emily said to Garrett.

He grinned at her, but his eyes quickly went to Summer who was panting behind Emily's head.

"Hey," he said.

Summer's cheeks instantly flushed. "Hey," she said back.

Emily looked back and forth between them, her grin growing bigger. "O. M. G. You two are adorable. It looks like things went well between the two of you."

"Emily," Summer said, her eyes intensely focused on her friend, obviously trying to convey some silent message. But Emily grinned innocently, obviously refusing to get that message.

"So..." Emily said looking back at Garrett and ignoring Summer. "What's the story?"

He frowned a little. "Story?"

"Story. Summer said you're going with her to the wedding, and if you all are going to show up at the wedding saying that you're her boyfriend, then there's obviously a story there. How you met, how's it going, all the good stuff. The rest of us, especially me, being her best friend, should be in on it, so we know what to say if people ask."

"You all are going to the wedding?" he asked.

Emily nodded. "Oh yeah. Our little group is more intermingled than a European royal family. Tony is Summer's boss and friend and Taylor's client, and his fiancée Janine works with Maggie which is how I became friends with her. Maggie introduced them at some party one of us threw a couple years ago."

"Ah," Garrett said, his head spinning a little. "And the story is because..."

"Because someone, or a lot of people, are going to ask. Weddings are boring as hell. Their divorce and the fact that they are both there with new people is going to cause some buzz."

"Wait," Maggie said, looking at Garrett. "You're going to the wed—"

Before she could finish, the screech of children echoed through the yard, and a tornado containing three little bodies came hurtling toward them. They were dressed in full climbing gear by were covered head to toe in mud. Apparently, they'd taken a dive or two into the mud pit under the monkey bars before hitting the climbing wall.

Josh brought up the rear, covered just as much, if not more than his children.

Emily smiled indulgently at them as they ran toward the table set up in the yard with snacks and water bottles. "Must be time for a refill," Maggie said.

The kids deposited their gear on the table and then hurtled themselves into their mother's arms, hugging her senseless and chattering excitedly about their adventures while Maggie doled out some food. As soon as she was done, the kids grabbed their goodies and ran off with a quick thank you.

Josh came over and wrapped an arm around his wife's waist while they watched their hyperactive offspring tearing around the yard before they disappeared into the course again.

Garrett chuckled. He'd grown up an only child and had always wondered what it would be like to have siblings to play with. Liam was probably the closest thing he had to a brother, and they hadn't met until after he'd joined the Army Ranger unit that Liam had commanded. He couldn't wait to have a big family of his own.

"I better get back out there before they attempt that rope bridge without me," Josh said, giving Emily a big kiss before grabbing a water bottle and heading back onto the course to play with his kids.

Garrett joined Emily in watching the kids play with what was probably a big goofy grin on his face. Summer handed Emily a towel off the table.

"Looks like you got a little something on you," she said.

Emily just laughed as she tried to brush at the mud splatters her offspring had left all over her, including a large handprint on her ass courtesy of Josh.

"Yeah, this is why I don't buy anything that cost more than ten bucks. It'll just get ruined anyway."

"And yet, you kept having more," Summer said, smiling at her friend.

"Yeah, well, they're kinda cute," Emily said, then shrugged. "They're a handful. They make me want to pull my hair out most days, and I'll never be able to own nice things until they've gone off for college. At which point, I still won't be able to afford nice things because we'll be paying three tuitions." She shrugged. "But it's worth it."

She aimed another motherly smile at the ball of dust that contained her children. Then closed her eyes with a cringe when a particularly loud shriek pierced the air. "I'll be deaf before I'm forty, but it's still worth it."

Summer just smiled and shook her head.

Interesting. Garrett watched her, wondering if she wanted kids or not. He wanted a big family. Always had. It hadn't occurred to him he'd ever be interested in a woman who didn't want kids, and he frankly wasn't all that sure what he'd do if that was the case with Summer.

He gave his head a little shake. He was getting *way* ahead of himself. Whether or not they each wanted kids wasn't exactly pre-date chit chat. Especially since she didn't seem to consider the date real.

With Josh and the kids back out of sight, Liam turned back to them. "Okay, so what was this about you coming to the wedding?"

"I'm Summer's date," he said, shooting a wink her way, his chest warming when her cheeks instantly flamed bright pink.

"He's more than that," Emily piped in. "They told Taylor that he was her boyfriend."

"What?" Maggie asked him, her eyes lighting up with a delighted grin.

Garrett shrugged but didn't say anything. It was the least he could have done.

Summer glanced up at him, and he gave her a faint shrug and nod. It was her story if she wanted to tell it. If not, he'd keep everything between the two of them. She was running this show.

She let out a long sigh. "Taylor was being his usual self..."

"Cockroach," Maggie muttered under her breath.

Summer's lips twitched. "Exactly. And Garrett was there and—I don't know what I was thinking—but I just..."

She stopped again, her cheeks flushing again, probably remembering that amazing kiss she'd laid on him that he couldn't stop thinking about. And she was obviously reluctant to tell her friends about it.

Unfortunately, they weren't going to leave it alone. But he was perfectly happy falling on that sword for her if it would make her more comfortable.

"I laid a big ol' kiss on her and told the dude I was her boyfriend," Garrett filled in.

Summer's surprised gaze shot to his, and she gave him a relieved smile. He winked at her again and turned back to their captive audience.

"I shouldn't have done it, but..."

"Hell yeah, you should have," Emily said. "I would have paid good money to see his face."

"It was pretty great, not gonna lie," Garrett said. "I should've taken a picture."

Summer sighed. "Yeah, I'll admit, I enjoyed it," she said with a little laugh. "But now poor Garrett is roped into going with me for the weekend, even though I told him he doesn't have to."

Garrett shrugged again. "Like I said, I don't have any other plans. I'm on leave for a few weeks, so I figured I'd come up to visit these guys. My schedule is wide open for a while and spending the weekend with a beautiful woman while knocking her ex down a peg or two sounds like a great time to me. In fact..." He grabbed her around the waist and pulled her against him. She squeaked adorably, and he grinned down at her. "I'm really looking forward to it."

She smiled and relaxed against him, letting him hold her. Annnd it was official. This is what heaven felt like.

Emily looked between the two of them with a huge, smug grin. Under normal circumstances, Garrett wouldn't have liked her meddling unless he specifically asked her to. But this time, the lady done good.

"So, you're doing the whole weekend? The bay cruise tomorrow night, all day festivities and wedding Saturday, breakfast thing on Sunday, all of it?"

Garrett's eyes widened a little. He hadn't known there was quite that much involved but, why the hell not? "Absolutely."

"Awesome! So...what's the story then?" Emily asked.

Summer sighed and pulled away from him, and he reluctantly let her go. For the moment.

"Let's just keep it simple and as close to the truth as possible. He's a friend of Liam's and I met him through Emily. Let's say three months ago, maybe?"

"Make it four months ago since I was actually on leave then," Garrett said. "Closer to the truth and provable if necessary."

Summer nodded. "Okay, sounds good. So, we met four months ago..."

"And hit it off right away," Garrett said, giving her a slow smile that made the color in her cheeks flare again. Damn, he loved when that happened. "I swept her right off her feet and still haven't set her back down."

Summer smiled and shook her head, ducking it a little. But she didn't argue.

Maggie looked back and forth between them, smiling, but still looking like she'd just gotten caught eavesdropping or something. "I think that's enough background to pass most cursory inquiries," she said. "We're just the friends, not actually in the relationship, so we wouldn't really need to know all the down and dirty details."

"Well maybe not *need* to know," Emily said, "but we sure as hell *want* to know."

Summer rolled her eyes. "There aren't any down and dirty details, Emily."

"Not yet," Emily said, flashing them a grin.

Summer threw her hands up. "You're impossible."

Emily just grinned. "Yeah, but you love me anyway."

"Lucky for you."

Liam laughed with the rest of them but came over to Garrett and clapped a hand on his shoulder. He drew him in a little so the ladies couldn't hear. "I'm glad you were there to put Taylor in his place. And I'm also glad Summer won't have to navigate the wedding by herself with that asshole there. But as her friend, I am under sworn duty..."

Garrett chuckled. "Yeah, yeah, you'll have my ass if I misbehave."

Liam smiled but his hand squeezed on Garrett shoulder. "You're damn right I will. Summer is an amazing woman and a good friend. I know this is all fake, but you better treat her right."

Garrett just shook his head. "I will absolutely treat her as she deserves to be treated, no matter what the circumstances. But this isn't fake for me."

Liam raised an eyebrow, and Garrett gave him a crooked grin. "I don't think it's fake for her either. She just needs to get over this hang-up she has with my age. But if I can talk her into dating me for real, I'm absolutely all in."

Liam nodded. "Well then, good luck to you. And just remember—"

"Yeah, I got it. She gets hurt, my ass is grass."

"Good man," Liam said with a smile.

Garrett just laughed and walked back over to where Summer stood watching the tangle of limbs that were Emily's kids. With Josh somewhere in the middle.

"Hey," he said, drawing her aside. "I've got to get going. I have a few things I need to tie up tonight and some appointments tomorrow. So, I probably won't be able to see you until right before the cruise. But how about I call you tonight and you can give me all the details."

Summer smiled a bit shyly at him but didn't hesitate to answer. "Okay, that sounds good."

"Good." Garrett held his hand out for her phone so he could enter his number into her contacts. "Shoot me a text so I've got your number."

"Gotcha," she said with a smile that made his breath stick in his throat.

He leaned in to kiss her cheek, inhaling her scent as he did. His eyes closed and he bit his lip to hold back a groan. She smelled incredible. Like...clean laundry and fresh country breezes. With a hint of faint floral. It was intoxicating. Somehow invigorating and calming all at the same time. Everything about her just felt...safe. Comforting. Like home. Something he hadn't had in a very long time.

"I'll call you around ten. Is that too late?"

"Nope, perfect," she said.

He took her hand and gave it a quick squeeze. "Perfect," he echoed, letting his gaze roam over her again. He started backing up, one step at a time, keeping her hand in his until he finally had to let go. But he walked backward a few more steps, keeping his gaze locked on hers for as long as he could. Until he had to turn around to walk or fall on his ass. Though hitting the pavement would have been worth it if he could have kept staring at her.

He could see the others watching them from his peripherals with varying looks of surprise and amusement, but he ignored them completely. She was all he cared about just then.

When he got to his truck, he climbed in, his heart pounding. He really hoped this weekend went well. Because if he couldn't convince Summer to date him for real, he was screwed. He was already obsessed, and they'd only just met. That thought should scare him a lot more than it did. But all he could think about was how much he was looking forward to seeing her the next evening. Hell, even just talking to her when she called tonight. And he *hated* talking on the phone.

There was no help for it. He had to make her his.

Chapter 7

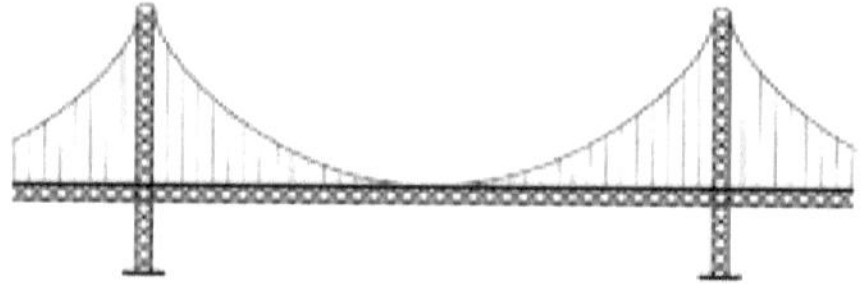

Summer sat tucked up in her bed, staring at the phone in her hand. She'd said she'd call him. And she wanted to. In theory. Making phone calls was one of the things that made her anxiety skyrocket. Too damn introverted. Even to call a guy who told her to call him.

She sighed and nearly jumped when her phone buzzed.

A text from Garrett.

Hey.

One tiny little word and she was grinning like one of those overly expressive Instagram dogs that were somehow both cute and creepy at the same time.

She took a deep breath and texted back.

Hey.

Smooooth.

You still going to call me?

Her thumb hovered over her screen for a second before she answered.

I could just give you all the info by text if you want.

She bit her lip and waited for his response.

You could...

Her shoulders slumped but before she could respond, more typing bubbles appeared.

But I'd really love to hear your voice.

And that did it.

Her heart still pounded, but now it was much more from anticipation than anxiety.

She hit the button to call him and put the phone on speaker.

"Hey," he said, the word sending happy little tingles throughout her body now that his voice was attached to it.

"Hey," she answered back.

"I'm glad you called."

And her heart stopped. "Me too."

"Didn't think you would for a minute."

She shrugged even though he couldn't see it. "I wanted to. I'm just a bit too introverted for my own good sometimes I think."

"I get that."

"You do?"

"Definitely. Especially when it comes to making phone calls. I hate making phone calls."

"Me too!" she said, grinning again.

"I hope you didn't feel like you had to call me. I wouldn't want..."

"No, not at all," she said. Then she took a deep, laughing breath, shaking her head and her own ridiculousness. "Don't mind me. We just don't know each other very well yet. I'm not so shy with people I know. Give it a few weeks. You won't be able to shut me up."

He chuckled. "Good to know."

Summer tried to think of something extra witty and sublimely flirty to say and...came up with nothing.

"So, what are you doing right now?" he asked.

She let out a relieved breath and got more comfortable, resting the phone on her chest. A nice rack came in handy sometimes. "Just watching a movie."

"Me too. What are you watching?"

"Uhhhh..." No way was she telling him.

"Come on, tell me. No judgement."

"Suuure."

"Come on. I'll tell you mine if you tell me yours."

She pursed her lips. Damn he was adorable. Fine. "It's a Brendan Fraser movie."

"Seriously?"

Here it comes. Taylor always gave her shit for the movies she loved. To him, the only worthwhile movies were action movies or horror. Because they made you think, apparently. About what, she had no clue. He probably didn't either. He just enjoyed making her feel like crap about the things she liked.

Given her past experience, she wasn't sure she wanted to hear the answer, but she asked anyway. "Yes, seriously. Why?"

"I'm watching one too."

Say what? "No way."

"Hey, Brendan Fraser is a damn god."

A happy little thrill bubbled through her. A man after her own heart. "No arguments here. I've loved everything I've ever seen him in."

"Right? He's an amazing action star, but he's like really funny, too. And definitely doesn't get enough respect for his romantic lead roles."

"Right?" Seriously, it was like Garrett was in her head. Which...yikes, kinda scary. But kind of nice, too. "Though I gotta be honest. It's a little weird to hear a guy raving about an actor's romantic chops."

"Hey, that's totally stereotyping. Guys can like romance."

"True. My bad." She waited a second and then added, "Though in my experience, most guys don't...or at least won't admit it."

Garrett snorted. "Maybe. You have met Liam, right?"

"Ha! Point taken." Liam and his romance novel collection was getting to be legendary. "So do you only like romance or are you into the action flicks too?"

"I like pretty much everything but horror."

Her eyes widened. "Really? A big, strong guy like you doesn't like horror?"

"Hell no. That shit'll keep me up at night."

She grinned. "I don't mind it too much."

"I've seen enough horror in my life," he added quietly.

She closed her eyes, mentally chastising herself for teasing him about it. She should have thought about what the man did for a living before making such a careless comment.

"I'm sorry," she murmured. "I didn't mean—"

"Nothing for you to apologize about," he said. "Just didn't want you thinking I was a total lightweight," he said, his voice back to its usual upbeat and teasing tone.

"Well, if it makes you feel any better, I definitely lean more toward the paranormal, creepy type stuff instead of the slasher serial killer movies. I'll take a homicidal ghost or vengeance-seeking vampire over a torturing serial killer any day."

"Yeah, I'd still nope right out of that whole list."

"Really?" she said with a laugh. "Not even something like *Twilight* or *Ghostbusters*?"

"Well, okay, that's different. Those are romantic vampires and funny ghosts. Which I'd still want to watch during daylight hours only please."

"Ha! I'll keep that in mind. Do I need to protect you from action movies too, or are those good?"

"Now those I like. For the most part. Until they start getting to the fourth or fifth sequel. Then it gets a little tedious. But generally, yes, action is good. But even those I like mixed with a good dose of humor or something. Like a Ryan Reynolds movie. Or, like Brendan Fraser. That's why he's so amazing. I mean, take *The Mummy*. Great action flick, for sure. It even has some horror elements with all the mummy stuff. But it's also probably the single best romance movie ever."

She sat up a bit, almost knocking her phone off her chest in her excitement. "Oh, totally agree. It's amazing! Also, and don't take this the wrong way, but it's a little weird having this convo with a tough guy army dude...wait...are you part of Liam's romance novel book club?"

There was a brief pause. "Well, it's not really Liam's club. It's run by a buddy across town. I mean, so I've heard..." he said, drawing the sentence out.

She sucked in a delighted breath. "Holy hell, you are." That was a layer she didn't expect to find.

"You say that like it's a bad thing," he said, chuckling.

"Okay, what is it with military men and romance novels?"

"I don't know why they get such a bad rap. I've never read a bad romance. Plus, I mean, they always have a happy ending...in more ways than one, if you get my drift."

"Oh, I get it."

"Hmmm, I bet you do," he said, his voice dropping to that range that made all the parts south of her navel tingle and tighten.

And then he continued right on like he hadn't just given her a waking wet dream with those four growly little words.

"Most of them have some great humor in them too. What's not to like?"

She sucked in a shaky breath. *Keep it together, woman!*

"Good points. So, you're a rom com guy, huh?"

"Hell yeah. Life is already too serious. I like my entertainment to cheer me up, not depress me more. Hence, the ban on horror."

"Ha! Gotcha."

"So..." he said. "You never said what movie you were watching."

She giggled and then slapped her hand over her mouth. She couldn't even remember the last time that sound had escaped her lips but there it was. Couldn't seem to help herself around him. "Neither did you."

"Okay...we say it at the same time."

"Okay. One...two...three..."

"*Mrs. Winterbourne*!" they said in unison.

She barked out a laugh. "I can't believe you're watching that!"

"In my defense, the movie choices on the channels available to me are sparce at the moment. But seriously, it's pretty fabulous. I mean it's no *George of the Jungle*, but—"

Her mouth dropped open. "No, I get it! *George of the Jungle* is amazing. And not just because Brendan looks amazing in a loin cloth."

"Hey. The man is more than just his loin cloth."

She raised a brow. "Are you accusing me of objectifying him?"

"No." His voice did that sexy, bedroom voice thing again and swear to God, her toes literally curled. "I'm just jealous you're thinking of him instead of daydreaming about *my* half-naked body."

All the air punched out of her chest, and it took her a second to get her bearings again. Because oh yeah, she could, and was, definitely imagining what Garrett would look like in nothing but a little loin cloth. And he'd absolutely give Brendan a run for his money.

"Who said I wasn't thinking of you too?" she finally managed.

His deep chuckle had her biting her lip.

"As long as I'm in there somewhere."

She tried to laugh again, but very little sound came out. "Garrett..." she said, his name a breathy plea on her lips.

He groaned, and she covered her eyes with her hand again. Not like that was going to help rescue her from the burning pool of desire that simple sound had tossed her in, but her brain couldn't seem to come up with any other defense mechanism other than *if I can't see you, I can't hear you.*

"Damn, woman, you say my name like that again, and I'm going to be outside your door in five seconds flat."

Oh, hell yes, please!

Wait. No. That would be bad. She couldn't remember why exactly just then but... No. Bad. Rinse. Repeat.

Say something!

But...way too many thoughts went skating through her head, and she couldn't say any of them. Thankfully, he rescued her with another question.

"So," he said, clearing his throat, "where does *Mrs. Winterbourne* rank on your Fraser Films of Fame?"

She took a deep breath and slowly blew it out, praying her voice came out normal. "One of my favorites, for sure. The first time I watched it, I literally hit play again the second it was over."

"Don't blame you. It's got everything. Romance, humor..."

"Blackmail, murder mystery..."

"Yes! Those too. See. Fabulous."

"Agreed. Oh! Wait..." She sat up again, her focus back on the television. "I love this scene."

They sat quietly, and she could hear the movie echoing from her phone as Brendan Fraser and Riki Lake danced through the kitchen before sneaking over to a doorway to check on his drunk butler.

"Tango!" She and Garrett both shouted along with the movie before dissolving into laughter and settling back to watch the characters' absolutely adorable first kiss.

"See?" Garrett asked. "Brendan is my hero."

Summer happy sighed and settled her phone back on her chest. "Ditto."

"So, fill me in on this weekend," he said.

Oops. She'd been having so much fun talking to him, she'd totally forgotten why she'd called him in the first place. Probably a good idea to tell him the details.

"Right! Sorry. Okay, so tomorrow night is the rehearsal dinner. We're taking a cruise around the bay. The boat leaves from Pier 3 at seven. And then Saturday, there's a picnic in the park event. Sort of a brunch type thing with some activities, I guess, starting at eleven. Then the wedding is at the San Francisco Mint at six."

"The Mint?"

She nodded, even though he couldn't see her. "It's got a really cool walled courtyard that just looks spectacular decked out with lights."

"That sounds amazing."

"It really is. I've been to some of their free concerts on Sundays, but never been to a wedding there. It's going to be gorgeous."

"I can't wait," he said, his voice warming, the tone implying it wasn't just the venue that he couldn't wait to see.

"And then, um..." *Breathe, just breathe.* "Sunday, they are doing a breakfast at nine so they can say goodbye to all their out-of-town guests. And then, you'll be free."

"Hmm, I'll have to eat slowly then."

She clenched her eyes shut again. Oh, heaven help her. So. Many. Inappropriate. Thoughts.

This was hands down her best phone call *ever*.

Chapter 8

Summer's quiet laugh skittered through Garrett's heart and sent it pounding. Such a simple sound, hardly audible, yet it had the power, it seemed, to make everything feel right in his world. He just needed to figure out how to convince her to let him in. She was interested, of that he had no doubt. Her response to his teasing...

He had to take a deep breath and will a little blood flow back toward his brain.

They watched the rest of the movie together, occasionally making comments. More often sitting in companionable silence, enjoying the film. So much so, that when it was over, they started another one. *The Mummy*, of course. By the time they were halfway through *The Mummy Returns*, her voice was growing sleepy on the other end of the line.

"Falling asleep on me?" he asked with quiet amusement.

"Nope, wide awake," she said, though she was obviously making an effort to perk up.

He chuckled. "We've been talking for about four hours now."

"We have?" she asked, her surprise evident in her voice.

"We have."

"It doesn't feel like it."

"Time flies when you're enjoying yourself."

She giggled and his lips immediately stretched into an answering smile. "That's not how that goes."

"No?"

"No."

"What is it then?"

"Time flies when you're having fun."

"Hmm. And are you having fun?"

He held his breath until she answered.

"Yes."

"You have no idea how much I like hearing you say that word," he said with another quiet laugh.

He had to bite off a groan when her breathy gasp echoed from the phone. She apparently liked it when his voice got low and deep. And he really, really liked that she liked it.

It was going to take an ice-cold shower before he'd be able to sleep tonight.

"Do you want to hang up?" he asked.

"No."

Relief and an almost overwhelming thrill of happiness flooded through him. "Good."

"Do you?"

"No."

"Good," she echoed back.

"But if you get too tired, let me know."

"Sure thing."

He shook his head grinning and turned his attention back to the movie. Where Rachel Weisz's character was kicking some serious tail.

"Evie is such a badass," he said.

"Hardcore," Summer agreed. "Such a change from the first movie."

"Naw, she was always a bit of a badass."

"Maybe, but in the first movie she was kind of mousy and quiet. Very proper, totally klutzy. Shocked by Rick and his brash American ways. By movie two, she's graduated from knocking over bookcases to headbutting people and holding her own in sword fights. It's cool, but it's almost like she's two different people."

"Hmm, interesting argument, go on."

"I mean, I'm not saying the changes aren't an improvement. I'd love to be half the badass she is."

"I think you're a total badass."

She snorted. "Thanks. I completely disagree but appreciate the vote of confidence."

He grinned. "You really don't give yourself enough credit. The fact that you managed to live with that ex of yours for so long without ending up on an episode of *Snapped* is seriously impressive."

He cringed. Just what every woman wanted to talk about with a potential new guy. Her asshat ex. Thankfully she laughed, and he relaxed a bit.

"It was a near thing some days, believe me. Living the single life has been heaven after living with him."

Garrett pursed his lips. That was not the direction he wanted this conversation to take. He couldn't blame her for feeling that way though. Taylor was enough to scare anyone off relationships. But he didn't want to talk about Taylor.

"So, you don't approve of the new and improved Evie?" he asked, trying to get things back on track.

"It's not that I don't approve...like I said, I like the new skills. It just seems like she's taken on her husband's personality or something."

He frowned. "Huh. Never thought of it that way before."

"I mean, it works great for the movie. But in real life, I don't think it usually works out so well when one partner changes so much for their spouse."

His frowned deepened. How much of this convo was about Evie and Rick and how much was about Summer and The Cockroach? He suspected it was much more about her than it was about the film characters.

He tried to think of how to word his response and finally just went for it. "I get your point. I mean, I've seen friends who change so much for their significant other there's almost nothing left of their own personality."

"So have I," she said, her voice quiet and pensive.

Oh yeah, she was definitely talking about herself. Kind of a heavy topic to be getting into with someone he barely knew. With anyone else, he probably would have left it alone. But he couldn't stand the sadness that permeated her voice even over through phone. And who was he kidding? He hadn't been able to leave her alone since the second he clapped eyes on her. Why start now?

"You know, I don't think that's always what's happening when people change in a relationship."

There was a pause before she answered. "What do you mean?"

"Well, like Evie," he said, pointing to the screen though she couldn't see him. "Yeah, she's definitely more outwardly badass. But I think that is more something that was always in her that Rick gives her the space and confidence to act on."

Another pause, but her voice was stronger when she answered. "Interesting argument, go on."

"She's really not all that different if you think about it. In the first movie, she was kinda quiet and klutzy, but she still dragged her brother into this huge adventure, talked Rick into helping them, negotiated with the corrupt prison guard to set him free, went on that whole quest, fought the bad guys and the mummies without going all fainting virgin on everyone, *and* tried to save everyone by willingly going with Imhotep. That takes balls."

"Hmmm, true."

"And in movie two, yeah, she's more confident and openly adventurous. But she's still a total nerdy librarian at heart. She's just in a healthy, loving relationship that makes her feel secure enough to really come into her own."

She was quiet again for another second. "I hadn't looked at it that way before, but I'll admit you make some valid points."

He smiled. "Still not totally convinced though, eh?"

"Let's just say I'm willing to concede that, provided you find the right partner, marriage might not be a total death trap."

He grinned and shook his head. It was a start. "That's a beautiful sentiment. Marriage isn't always a death trap. You should use that in a wedding toast tomorrow."

"Ha! I'm classy enough to keep my opinions on marriage to myself. On special occasions anyway."

He chuckled and then took a deep breath and blew it out. And asked the question that was burning in his gut. "So, you think you'll ever give it another try?"

"Marriage?" she asked quietly.

"Yeah." He held his breath. Her long sigh made him release it as a hard lump of disappointment settled in his chest.

Not that he had any right to it. He didn't even know her middle name yet. Why the hell was he fantasizing about changing her last name? If he didn't get a grip, there was a very good possibility she'd stomp all over his heart.

"I don't know. It's..." She sighed again.

His chest tightened. Crazy or not, at the moment, he was willing to get his heart stomped on for just the chance it would heal hers a bit.

"To be totally honest, no. I don't see myself ever getting married again."

He couldn't help but ask. "Even if you find the right partner?"

"But that's the problem, isn't it? You might be absolutely convinced the one you're marrying *is* the right partner. Why else would you be marrying them? But maybe they've been hiding things. Maybe you're hiding things. Maybe things change down the road. How do you know until it's too late?"

He wasn't sure what to say to that. She wasn't wrong. But he was afraid if he agreed, she'd use it as an excuse to keep him at arm's length and that was the last thing he wanted.

"You're right, you don't ever know for sure," he finally said. "But if you never take a chance, you could be missing out on something amazing."

Her quiet sigh filtered to him through the phone, and he wished he was lying next to her so he could pull her into his arms. What was this woman doing to him?

"You're right," she said. "But still...let's just say it's definitely not something I'm ready for right now."

"Fair enough," he said, biting his tongue to keep from trying to talk her over to the wedded bliss side. Talking wouldn't help. And, as he apparently needed to keep reminding himself, it was incredibly premature anyway.

He blamed it on his parents. They'd met online and had been engaged on their second phone call. They were still going strong almost three decades later. Sometimes when you knew, you knew. And he was pretty sure he knew.

It wasn't love at first sight...not really. He didn't know her well enough to love her. But it was more like...potential at first sight. If she'd give them a chance.

He'd just have to show her that relationships could be amazing, if you were with the right person.

They kept watching the movie, making a few comments here and there, until he heard faint snores coming from the other end of the phone.

He laughed. "Summer?" he asked quietly. "Summer?"

The only response was a louder snore and some slight mumbling. That sounded very much like, "G'night, Gare."

And damn if that didn't hit him right in his happy place. Shit, the woman was more than half asleep and miles away and still had the power to render him breathless with two little half-spoken words.

"Goodnight, Gorgeous," he said, keeping his voice low. "I'll see you tomorrow."

Tomorrow, he was going to start proving to her that he was worth taking a chance on. He'd never looked so forward to anything in his life.

Chapter 9

Summer had the Uber driver pull up to the main pier entrance instead of going to the parking lot at the boat landing. She needed the few extra minutes. And she didn't want to be in sight of the boat full of her friends while she sat having an existential crisis in the back of a Ford Focus while going through her pros and cons list of getting out of the car for probably the hundredth time since they'd left her house. There were a lot of cons. Quite a few pros also though. The biggest being she got to see Garrett again. However, that was also the biggest con. She liked him far too much for taking this any farther to be a good idea.

Her divorce was still pretty fresh. She was just starting to get used to being single again. To figure out who she was without The Cockroach. Things were going great at work, and it finally felt like she was starting to get her life in order. The last thing in the world she needed was some messy fling with a younger man.

A one-night stand...maybe. She'd never really indulged in those before and frankly they sounded like a lot of fun. String-free sex? With a guy who would hopefully not get off and then promptly fall asleep without bothering to check if she'd even remotely enjoyed herself. How refreshing, not to mention satisfying, would that be?

But Garrett was not one-night stand material. He had relationship written all over him, and she wasn't ready for that yet. Didn't know if she ever would be. So, it wouldn't be fair to get into anything with Garrett when she was a hundred percent...okay, maybe ninety-nine percent...sure things wouldn't work out.

Hence her still sitting in the car, hand on door handle, unable to decide whether to stay or go.

"Ma'am?" Joe, the driver, said. "Was this where you wanted to be dropped off? I can take you up to the landing parking lot. They won't charge if I'm just dropping off. Or...did you want me to take you somewhere else?"

She met his gaze in the rearview mirror, her cheeks burning. "Yeah. I mean, no. I'm sorry. I'm staying."

But she still didn't open the door. She needed to. Garrett was on that boat full of her friends and colleagues waiting for her. No matter what crazy thoughts were going through her head, she couldn't just ditch him. He'd be with their friends, but still. That would be unforgivable when the only reason he was there was to help her. She needed to get her ass out of the car and onto that boat.

She blew out a frustrated breath. "Sorry," she said again. Then she laughed a little. "I don't know why I'm making such a big deal out of this. It's just my friend's rehearsal dinner. It's not like we're going to be alone or anything. And even if we were, it's not like this is a real date or anything, right?"

Joe's eyebrows hit his hairline. "No?"

She nodded. "No. He's just pretending to be with me so my shithead ex won't have satisfaction of me showing up alone while he's there with his new model girlfriend."

"Ah. That's nice of him."

"Right? So, me not showing up when he's gone through all this trouble to save my ego would be a really shitty thing to do."

"True."

She nodded again. "Right. Okay."

But she still didn't open the door. "I mean I know why this feels like such a big deal." She snorted. "It's because this guy isn't just some random guy that I'll forget about come Monday morning, you know?"

Joe turned sideways so he could look at her face instead of her reflection. "He's not?"

She shook her head. He was the guy that had been invading her dreams all night not to mention most of her waking thoughts since the moment he'd walked into her house lugging Taylor's box of crap and sporting an adorable grin that she would probably see every time she closed her eyes for the rest of her life.

She sighed and leaned forward so she could lower her voice. Not like anyone else could hear them. "I like him. A lot."

Annnd she'd just said it out loud, so now it was real. It was *out there* in the universe. No backsies. She groaned and dropped her head onto the back of the seat in front of her.

"So...wouldn't it be better to go on this date then?" Joe asked. "Or do you not think he feels the same way?"

She shook her head again. "No, he does. He's made it very clear he wants this to be for real. We even talked for like five hours last night, and I didn't get bored once."

Joe flung out a hand. "Well, there you go, then. You should definitely go on the date."

She sighed again. "I know. But...I don't know. It's like something's telling me that if I walk onto that boat, I'm going to be leaving without my heart, you know?"

He grinned. "That's a great feeling. Especially if it works out."

She smiled faintly. "Yeah. But...I'm just not sure I'm ready for that yet. I just got divorced."

"Ah," he said, nodding knowingly.

"I mean, theoretically it's been long enough. The divorce hasn't been final all that long, but we split months ago. And my ex has certainly moved on already. But...I don't know. I've never really been alone, and I've kind of been enjoying it."

"I get that. But you don't want to be alone forever."

She frowned. "No. But then again, I'm not sure I'm really ready to throw a new guy in the mix just yet."

He nodded again. "You're putting too much pressure on yourself. This is just a date. Just go have fun."

She nodded slowly. "Yeah. No harm in just having some fun, right?"

"Right." He glanced out the window and his eyes grew wide. "Is that him?"

Summer jerked her head around to look in the direction Joe had nodded and caught sight of a devastatingly hot Garrett, clad in expertly tailored dark gray slacks, his silver button up shirt fitted to perfection, his monochromatic gray tie accentuating his sculpted chest, patiently waiting a few yards from the car. He'd even rolled up the sleeves of his shirt, exposing his forearms. Why that was so damn sexy, she had no idea. It just *did* it for her. And pretty much every other woman she knew.

"It's just not fair for anybody to look that good," she murmured.

Joe snorted. "Good? Honey, he's a straight up snack."

That startled a laugh out of her. Garrett bent down a little so he could look at her through the window. Which gave him a perfect view of her staring at him. He cocked an eyebrow with a half grin that was almost shy.

She let out tremulous sigh. "Yeah, he is. Absolutely delicious."

Joe chuckled. "Okay, I know you say you aren't ready but..."

She snorted herself. "I know. I'm an idiot."

"Yeah."

"Okay. I'm getting out."

"I would."

She smiled. "Thanks for the talk."

"Any time," he said with an answering grin. "Hey, do me a favor. Call me up next time you need a ride. I want to see how things turned out."

She laughed again. "Deal." She put her hand back on the door handle and took a deep breath. "Okay. Here goes nothing."

"Good luck," Joe said.

"Thanks." Then she pulled the handle and stepped out of the car before she could change her mind.

"Hey there," Garrett said, coming over to her. "Wasn't sure you were going to get out of the car there for a second."

She gave him a tremulous smile. "Wasn't sure myself there for a second."

"Hmm," he said, reaching up to run his hands down her arms. She shivered at the sensation but stepped closer to him instead of pulling away. "Why is that?" he asked, his voice dropping an octave.

She shivered again, every nerve ending in her body lighting up. She closed her eyes and put her hands against his chest, breathing deep, bathing in his scent. His warm hands wrapped around her arms and drew her closer, and she dropped her forehead to his chest.

"Because I like you," she said, half hoping he wouldn't hear her. The sudden tension in the muscles under her fingers belayed that hope though.

"Summer."

She kept her head down and he chuckled.

"Look at me."

She took a deep breath...and couldn't quite lift her head.

His fingers gently wrapped around her chin and lifted her face until she met his smiling gaze. "I like you, too."

Her breath left her in a rush, and he leaned down, pulling her face to his.

She had half a breath to second guess herself before his lips met hers and all other thoughts evacuated. There was nothing left but him. His soft lips molded to hers; his arms wrapped around her and held her close as she rose on her toes to deepen the kiss. All the uncertainty, all the mental gymnastics, all the pain and confusion and stress of the last several months—hell the last several years—just disappeared into wave of need that gripped her so tight nothing else registered.

Her hands cupped the back of his head, her mouth moving over his, taking what she'd needed for so long. And he followed her right over the edge, giving her everything she'd been craving. Everything she hadn't even known she'd been missing.

Sweet. Holy. *Hell.* The man could kiss.

The sound of her phone blaring from her purse jolted them out of the moment, and they just stared at each other for a second, frowning in confusion while they dragged in lungfuls of ragged breaths.

Then her phone went off again and Garrett laughed while she fumbled for it. There was a text from Emily.

The boat is about to leave. Move it!

"Shit! We're going to miss the boat."

Garrett just grinned. "Worth it."

Summer beamed up at him, and he took her hand.

"We better run for it," he said. "Ready?"

She nodded and took off with him, running on the balls of her feet to keep from breaking a heel while they hauled ass across the pier to where the boat was docked. Their friends on the upper deck hooted and hollered at them as they barreled across the gangplank just in time.

They paused just inside, and Summer slapped a hand to her chest, trying to keep her racing heart from pounding through her chest. "Oh my God, I haven't run that fast in...well, ever," she said with a slight wheeze. "And you're not even winded."

She mock-glared at Garrett, who grinned and wrapped an arm around her waist. "True, but then again, I didn't have to run in heels."

"Hmm, sure, that's totally the difference," she said.

"Hey," Maggie said, coming over to them with Liam and company in tow. "We didn't think you guys would make it. What kep—"

Maggie stopped, her face splitting into a huge grin. "Never mind."

"What?" Summer asked, putting a hand to her hair. She couldn't be that windblown, could she?

Emily moved so she could get a better look and laughed. "You two might want to step into the restroom for a moment and um...freshen up."

Summer took a better look at Garrett and her cheeks instantly flooded with heat. He cocked an eyebrow at her, then gave her a crooked little grin that sent her heart skittering about her chest.

He rubbed his thumb under her bottom lip. "I guess your lipstick got a little smeared..."

Emily snorted. "That's probably because you're wearing more of it than she is."

He rubbed at his own lips. "Is it my color?"

Summer couldn't contain her smile. "Everything is your color."

He winked at her. "Maybe I'll leave it on then."

Emily rolled her eyes and pushed them both toward the bathrooms. "Go get cleaned up. Then meet us on the casino deck. Mama's got some college tuitions to fund."

"I don't think you can win any actual money, Em," Maggie said. "I believe it's just a 'for fun' type casino."

"Ugh. Where's the fun in that?" Emily rolled her eyes. "Whatever. You two, go, clean up. Janine and Tony are out on the upper deck—you should probably say hi at some point so they know you made an appearance—and we will be pretending we can win some actual cash."

Summer laughed again, her eyes lingering on Garrett as they both pushed into the bathrooms.

That particular shade of mauve really was his color.

One glance in the mirror over the sink showed her exactly why her friends were so amused. Her lipstick was pretty much non-existent except for the nice halo effect she had going on, especially under her bottom lip. So freaking embarrassing.

But...kinda hot too. It had been a very long time since anyone had been so involved in kissing her that they left her face a smeared mess. Here's to hoping it would happen again. Very soon. In fact, maybe she should stick to a nice gloss instead of the deep mauve she'd been wearing. Just in case.

She pulled the small travel pack of makeup remover wipes from her purse, wincing in sympathy at the sounds of someone tossing their cookies in the stall behind her.

"You okay in there?" she asked, watching the door in the mirror while she cleaned up her face and tried to decide between the clear gloss or lipstick.

She finally went with the lipstick but applied a lighter coat as a compromise. She didn't want to be too obvious that she was ready and waiting for another make-out session.

The door to the stall opened and a gorgeous blonde came out with her hand over her mouth, looking more than a little green around the gills.

"Yeah, I'm okay," she said, staggering to the sink and flipping on the cool water. "Just a little seasick."

"Ah," Summer said, opening her purse again. "I know how you feel." She pulled out a motion sickness pill and handed it to the woman. "Here, try this. I never step foot on one of these boats without these babies," she said with a sympathetic smile. "It does take thirty minutes or so to kick in though, so you might want to stop by the bar and grab a club soda or ginger ale. And then go sit on the upper deck in the fresh air. That really helps."

"Thank you," the woman said, taking it gratefully. "I wanted to stop and get some on the way here, but my boyfriend didn't want to risk being late. I hate boats."

"Yeah, they definitely take some getting used to."

The other woman shook her head. "Ugh, never again. I'm just counting the hours until this floating nightmare docks, and then I'm never setting foot on another one."

Summer smiled at her again. "I don't blame you. I hope you feel better," she said, slinging her purse back over her shoulder.

The woman gave her a faint smile. "Thanks..."

"Summer," she said. But her grin froze halfway on her lips as the woman's face blanched.

"Summer?"

Summer nodded, taking a wary step back. She didn't want to be in the splash zone if the woman's lunch was about to make another reappearance. "Laurent," she added.

The woman's face took on a bit of a greenish shade that worried Summer. "I..." Her forehead crinkled, and she sucked in a shaky breath. "I really need to get some air."

She rushed for the door, calling another hasty thank you over her shoulder as she disappeared.

Summer frowned after her, then shrugged, checked her face in the mirror one more time, and went back out to find Garrett.

Who stood right outside the door waiting for her.

His face broke into a brilliant grin when he caught sight of her. "There you are. I was starting to think you'd crawled out the window and made a swim for it."

Summer chuckled. "Sorry. Got a little held up trying to help some poor woman with a bad case of motion sickness."

"Ah," he said, holding out his elbow for Summer to take. Um, swoon. "Was that the blonde that ran out the door right before you came out?"

"Yeah. She said she was going to get some air."

"Good. I hope she feels better. Because *we* are about to have an amazing night." He pulled his elbow into his side, drawing her close.

"Oh, we are, are we?"

"Absolutely," he said, leaning down to brush a careful kiss across her lips.

For a split second, that nagging inner voice in her head that seemed bound and determined to ruin her life started up again.

He's too young.

You barely know him.

What would everyone think of us?

Of me? Of...

Ugh. She was about sick of her inner nag. It needed to STFU. Because the hottest guy on the planet was gazing down at her like she was the last warm Krispy Kreme cronut in the box and she was all his to devour, and she was *so* down for that and tired of pretending otherwise. It might only last the one night. Or if the universe was kind, the entire weekend. And then he might be gone. And frankly it was for the best of all involved if that was the case, so she'd do her damned level best to make sure this stayed casual.

But for once in her pathetic life, she was going to grab an amazing opportunity by the balls and have some fucking fun. Pun one thousand percent intended.

She stretched up on her toes to kiss him again and then smiled. "Sounds good to me. Let's go."

Chapter 10

"Did they say there was a casino on this boat?" Garrett said, lacing his fingers through Summer's as they made their way through the crowd.

The sensation of her warm skin sliding against his had his belly tightening and he had to take a nice slow breath to get a grip. It was going to be an extremely long night if he had to excuse himself to the restroom every time she brushed against him. Even so, he couldn't help but rub his thumb over her knuckles.

"Yep."

He smiled at her less-than steady voice. Good to know he wasn't the only one affected.

"I mean it's not Vegas," she continued. "But they've got a pretty decent offering. See?"

They stopped in the large, arched doorway and took in the scene. "Wow, nice."

Dealers in bowties and white tuxedo shirts held court over craps tables, blackjack, roulette, and pretty much anything else you'd want to play while touring San Francisco Bay in a big boat.

"But I'm pretty sure Maggie was right, and you can't win actual money," she said. "You just play with chips and have fun."

"Too bad. There's our group," he said, chuckling as he pointed out Emily madly waving at them from a craps table.

"Oh God," she said, spotting someone else.

"Wha—" Garrett looked at her, concern filling him at the tone of her voice. "Oh," he said, spotting Taylor a few seconds after she did.

Taylor stopped in front of them, two drinks in his hands. His eyes did a quick perusal and if Garrett wasn't mistaken, a spark of appreciation flashed through his eyes as he looked at his ex-wife. The look was gone too quick to be sure and soured the instant it turned on Garrett. But Garrett would be willing to bet money—the real stuff, not the 'for fun' cruise stuff—that Taylor wasn't nearly as unaffected by Summer as he liked to pretend.

Good. He brought Summer's hand, still entwined with his, up to his lips, enjoying the ripple of irritation on Taylor's face. And the shiver of pleasure that went through her if her trembling hand was any indication.

"Summer," Taylor said.

"Taylor."

She stood watching him, not giving him anything but a pleasant smile though her hand was squeezing Garrett's like he was her lifeline.

He didn't know what Taylor had expected but whatever it was, he didn't get it, so he turned his attention to Garrett with a scowl.

"Are you even old enough to be in here?" he asked.

Garrett just smiled at him though a thread of anger started building in his gut. "Yes. Just barely," he said, winking at him. "Though since it's not a real casino it probably doesn't matter."

Taylor opened his mouth to spew some more nastiness, but Summer cut in. "Where's your date this evening?"

Ha. Touché. Though Summer was probably just asking to make conversation, Garrett couldn't help but enjoy her pointing out that Taylor was standing there alone while she was most definitely with someone.

Taylor scowled again. "She's upstairs freezing her ass off on the upper deck. Apparently, she gets seasick." He grimaced like he couldn't believe she had the temerity to have a weakness. "She wanted some fresh air and a ginger ale," he said holding up one of the drinks. "I'm sure she'll be feeling better in a few minutes."

"I hope so," Summer said, sounding completely genuine. She certainly didn't look anything but totally sincere. She was a good woman. Taylor didn't deserve her.

"Well," she said, "we'll see you around, I'm sure. We're going to go join our group." She nodded over to where Liam, Maggie, Emily, and Josh stood not even pretending they weren't staring at them.

Taylor nodded at them, and Emily gave a jaunty wave that ended with her flipping him the bird. Though he turned away just as she did it. Garrett tried to turn the laugh that escaped his throat into a cough, though it didn't work very well. Summer grabbed his arm, a giggle escaping her own lips.

"Bye, Taylor," she said, turning her back on him and steering Garrett over to their waiting friends.

"Holy hell, I thought I was going to lose it right in front of him," she said with a shaky laugh. "Emily, seriously, behave yourself." She gave her friend a little push but was obviously too amused for the admonition to really mean anything.

Emily just snorted. "That *was* behaving myself."

Garrett glanced at Josh who nodded. Garrett chuckled and tugged on Summer's hand to draw her to the table.

"Come on, Summer. Let's win some fake money."

She flashed a grin at him that lit his soul on fire, and he had to grip the table in front of him to keep from grabbing her and hauling her off to some dark corner somewhere. Not that he could see any dark corners. Though there was a distinct thump of bass coming from somewhere on the boat. If there was a dance floor somewhere, he and Summer were going to get their freak on as soon as possible.

In the meantime, she was proving to be his good luck charm. He'd only played craps one other time, right after he'd turned twenty-one and had been able to go into a casino for the first time. He'd sucked at it. Well, it was kind of hard to suck at something that required one hundred percent luck and zero skill. But he'd been decidedly unlucky.

This time, however, everything he threw was golden. With Summer at his side, though, he never had any doubt.

He leaned over to grab the dice again and held his fist up to Summer like every cheesy Vegas movie scene he'd ever seen, waggling his eyebrows. "Give me some good luck, baby."

She rolled her eyes but obligingly blew on his dice. He winked at her and then threw them. The whole table went wild when he hit a seven for the third time in a row.

"I can't believe you just won again!" Summer said.

He pulled her in for a hug. "I can. You're my lucky charm."

She shook her head, her cheeks flushing red, but she was smiling so he took that for a good sign.

"Too bad it's not real money," she said.

He groaned. "Seriously. I don't think I even want to know how much I've got sitting there," he said, gesturing to his pile of fake chips. "It'll be too depressing that it's not real."

"We should probably go see if we can find Tony and Janine," she said, leaning in so he could hear her over the rest of the crowd. "I need to go say hi."

He nodded and took her hand again. He kept expecting her to pull her hand away or at least to drop it when they came near someone she knew. Despite what she said about not being embarrassed to be seen with him, he knew she wasn't totally comfortable. Though that had more to do with her age hang up than it did with him personally, he knew. Still. Every time she happily threaded her fingers through his, a fuzzy, happy warmth wound its way from their entwined hands straight through his chest.

Kissing her had set him on fire. But holding her hand...that made him want to skip through the countryside with all his woodland friends whilst singing of dreams coming true.

Summer led him to the upper deck where the bride and groom were holding court in the middle of a group of their friends. Taylor included.

Garrett glanced at Summer, making sure she was okay. But aside from a momentary hesitation, she pushed ahead.

"Janine!" she said, throwing her arms around the bride.

"You made it! Taylor said he wasn't sure if you were coming."

"Did he?" Summer asked with a small frown.

Jag-off. He knew damn well Summer was going, even before he found out about Garrett.

Janine looked like she just realized she may have said something that could start an incident, especially with Taylor standing nearby with his miserable, still slightly green date.

But Summer waved it off with a smile. "Of course, I was coming. My boss would probably fire me if I missed your rehearsal dinner." She raised an eyebrow at Tony, who just grinned and leaned forward to air-kiss her cheek.

"Glad you could make it," he said.

Janine caught sight of Garrett and raised her eyebrows. "And who is this?"

Summer's smile grew shier, but she didn't hesitate to pull him closer. "This is my boyfriend, Garrett Vogel. Garrett, this is the bride, Janine, and her fiancé—and my boss—Tony."

They exchanged the usual pleasantries though Garrett could tell Janine was dying to take Summer aside and get some details. He grinned and gave Summer's hand a squeeze.

They stepped back to give other people access to the couple of honor and turned right into Taylor and Carolina.

Taylor glanced at him coldly and turned his attention to Summer. “Summer, this is my girlfriend, Carolina Burchek.” He placed extra emphasis on the word girlfriend and Garrett gritted his teeth, trying to keep his anger dialed down to a minimum. The Cockroach seemed to enjoy trying to rile Summer up. But...

Garrett glanced at Summer and couldn’t help the smile that broke out. The woman was amazing. Really. Not a trace of any emotion but polite concern was on her face when she ignored Taylor completely and leaned toward Carolina, reaching out to lightly grasp her arm.

“How are you feeling? Has the pill kicked in yet?”

Carolina smiled at her gratefully. “I think so. I am starting to feel a bit better. And the ginger ale and fresh air really helped. Thanks.”

Summer smiled again. “My pleasure. I’m glad you’re feeling better.” She spared her ex only the briefest of glances as she turned to leave. “Taylor,” she said with a small nod.

And then they were walking away. Her hand trembled a bit in his, but she kept walking until they turned the corner, out of Taylor’s sight.

Then he couldn’t hold it back any longer. He pulled her to a stop then into his arms for a bear hug.

She yipped a little and then laughed, wrapping her arms around his shoulders.

He set her back on her feet after a few seconds and took her face in his hands. “At the risk of sounding ridiculous...I’m proud of you. You handled that perfectly.”

Her smile grew. “I’m pretty proud of myself too.” Her hands slipped down to his chest, and she played with his tie while she spoke. “I’ve been dreading running into him with everyone we know around. Especially with his new girlfriend on his arm. But...it wasn’t so bad. To be honest, I mostly just feel sorry for her.”

She gave him a little half grin and shrugged. “And as for him...” She let out a long breath. “For the first time in a long time, I didn’t really care about him or his opinion at all.”

Garrett beamed down at her, filled to the brim with pride at this incredible woman he was lucky enough to be with. For the moment, at least. Longer if he could talk her into it. And the more time they spent together, the better he was starting to think his chances were.

The thumping bass coming from the next deck down filtered up to them again, and she turned to him with a mischievous grin he'd never seen on her before.

"Let's go dance."

He laughed. "Ah yeah, baby. Take me to your dance floor."

Chapter 11

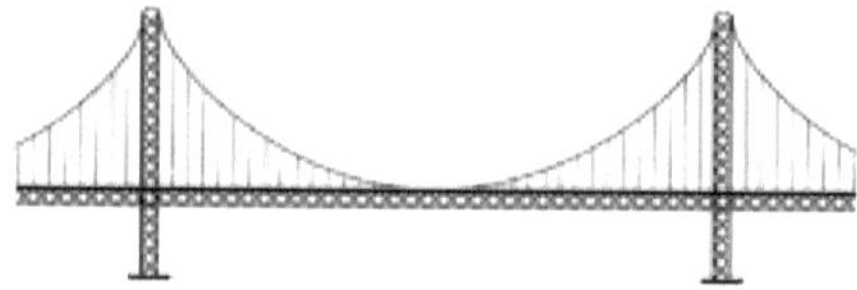

It only took about thirty seconds into the first song before Summer realized she'd made a huge mistake.

Dancing with Garrett was...hot. Too hot. Scorching hot. They'd barely done more than a couple of middle-schoolers at their first dance. Nothing but putting their hands fairly chastely on each other and swaying to the music. But holy hell. She didn't know if it was the steady pulse of the music echoing in her veins, the clublike atmosphere made somehow more intimate with the gorgeous view of the bay from outside of the windows, or the fact that she was pressed against the hottest guy in the room—or some combo of the three—but she was about ready to throw down some serious PDA. And she was not a public display of affection person. Hell, she was rarely a private display of affection person. Under normal circumstances.

Then again, she'd been with Taylor for years. Affection wasn't really part of his vocabulary. And, unlike her dealings with The Cockroach, no circumstance that included Garrett was a normal circumstance.

The tempo changed as the song morphed into something faster and Garrett grinned, letting go of her so he could dance backwards a few steps. He didn't go far though before he held out a hand and drew her in, singing along with the music. She followed his lead, unable to help herself.

He was a surprisingly good dancer. He didn't just hold her close and grind on her. Though she would have been more than happy to go along with *that* ride. In fact, she danced a little closer, hoping to spark a little something.

He gave her that slow sexy grin that had her insides spinning like Cirque de Soleil and pulled her close, his hand pressed to the small of her back. He brought her hand up and held it against his chest as they turned. She buried her face in his neck, inhaling deeply, and he let his cheek caress hers as he moved his head.

They'd barely moved but her heart was pounding like she'd just climbed aboard the boat after swimming to it from the shore.

He lifted his head and grinned. And then took a firm grip of her hand and spun her out before pulling her back in with an elegant twirl. Her laughter erupted before she could stop it. She'd never been twirled in her life.

"Where did you learn to dance like this?" she asked.

He just smiled and twirled her again. "Summer camp," he said, when she made it back to his chest.

"Really?"

He chuckled. "Naw. Dated a girl in college who was a dance major. I was homework."

"Lucky girl," Summer said.

"Hmm," he said, holding her close. He ran the tip of his nose along her jawline, nuzzling her. "Lucky me."

She looked up at him, startled.

"Ready for another spin?" He winked at her and sent her twirling out again.

Only this time she made the mistake of paying attention to something outside her little bubble with Garrett. And saw her friends sitting at a nearby table, all watching the show. The only thing they were missing were tubs of popcorn. Actually, Josh and Liam *were* sharing a bowl of pretzels or something. When they saw her notice them, they all cheered.

Oh God.

Garrett tugged on her hand, pulling her back in. Only this time, it didn't go so smoothly. She spun in okay. But instead of keeping her arm in close, that bad boy was flapping in the wind like a blow-up puppet in front of a car dealership. Not ideal when you're spinning into your partner.

Her hand connected with Garrett's nose and a sharp pain shot up her arm. He grunted and slapped a hand over his nose. But not before Summer saw a bright trickle of red.

"Oh my God!" She grabbed his free hand and pulled him from the crowd. He kept his head tilted back, seemingly trusting her to get him clear. You'd think he'd have learned his lesson about trusting her since she was the one who clocked him in the first place.

She got him to her friends' table, shooing Josh out of his chair so Garrett could sit.

At least she could say one thing about her group of friends. They might enjoy teasing and meddling and being a general nuisance, but they were cool and calm and willing to help in a crisis.

Maggie and Emily got the men out of the way and produced glasses of ice water and napkins from somewhere. Summer didn't care, she was just grateful to have something to hold against Garrett's nose. Even though he kept laughing and trying to push her away.

"Summer," he said, chuckling again when he failed another attempt to dodge an ice-filled napkin she shoved against his nose. "I'm fine, I promise. It's not even bleeding anymore, see?"

He moved the napkin long enough for her to see that he wasn't permanently damaged. In fact, there was no swelling or redness at all, so whatever she'd done, it hadn't been horrible. She breathed a sigh of relief and sagged against the table.

"I'm so sorry," she said.

He tried to take her hand, but she evaded him a few times before he managed to grab it. Embarrassment flooded her. Of all the stupid things to do. Oh sure, let's just go flinging our arms about like there's no one else in the room who might not enjoy getting the shit smacked out of them.

"Hey," he said, probably not for the first time. "It's really okay. Come here."

She just looked at him. "Seriously? You want me to get closer?"

"Always." The smile he gave her had her stomach pulling an Olympic gymnast-worthy triple backflip loop de loop.

She reluctantly let him pull her until she stood between his legs. He tugged on her hand but there was no way she was going to sit on his lap. She'd crush his poor leg and then he'd not only have to leave the room with a probably ready-to-re-bleed-at-any-moment nose but a hobbled leg as well.

"Summer," he said, the quiet command in his voice breaking through her self-indulgent pity party. "Come here."

She sat, her breath leaving her in a rush. Damn. Yes, *sir*. And say it again please.

This time she didn't fight him when he pulled her against his chest. She buried her face in his neck and let him hold her.

Nothing—*nothing*—had ever felt so good.

"What's going on?" he murmured to her. "You seem a lot more upset than a bumped nose should call for."

She breathed in his sharp, clean scent and let it all out in a slow rush. "I don't know. I guess I just expected...I mean if I had done that to..."

She choked out a laugh. Man. Taylor had really done a job on her, hadn't he?

She shook her head. "I guess old habits just die hard."

He wrapped both his arms around her and kissed the top of her head. And he just...held her. He didn't rush her. Or chastise her. Or throw a fit because their night was ruined. They just sat quietly, his arms around her, and watched their friends have a blast. He held her until her body went limp with relaxation. Until her mind had cleared of anything unpleasant. Until she snuggled against him with a happy sigh and whispered, "Thank you."

He kissed her temple. "Any time."

He leaned his forehead against her and after a few moments she could feel it crinkle in a frown. "I've been meaning to ask...what kind of a wedding rehearsal dinner is this?"

With her sitting on his lap, she could look right into his deep brown eyes. His nose was a bit red on the bridge, but there was no blood and no swelling or bruising that she could see. Hallelujah.

"It's more of a party, I guess, than an actual rehearsal. We did a quick run through of the ceremony earlier this morning at the Mint. But Janine and Tony didn't want to do a normal dinner at some fancy restaurant. Our graduating class did one of these cruises after our college graduation, and it was a blast, so they thought it would be fun to do one instead of a typical dinner."

He nodded. "It's definitely more fun than some boring restaurant. I'll have to keep it in mind."

She glanced at him in surprise.

He raised his brows. "What?"

She shrugged. "I don't know. I didn't think guys did that."

"Did what?"

"The whole planning a hypothetical future wedding thing."

"Hmm, well maybe you don't know as much about guys as you thought."

She snorted. "Oh, that's a given. And seeing as how I'm pretty sure I know next to nothing, that tells you how much I know about guys."

"Well, there's really only one guy I care about you knowing, so it's all good."

Her heart pounded so hard she had to suck in a breath to keep her lungs working. "Oh really?"

He nodded, pursing his lips together. "Oh yes. I am the most important. Ask anyone."

She shook her head with a smile. "You give the term 'delusions of grandeur' a whole new meaning."

"I do aim for perfection."

She brought her hand up to his cheek. She knew he was joking but... "You're pretty damn close."

He stared at her, his eyes searching hers until her breath went ragged.

How did he do that with nothing but a look?

She leaned closer to him; barely aware she was doing it. Then he lifted his knee slightly, enough that it made her slide closer to his chest. Until their faces were inches apart. Their lips nearly touching. Their eyes still locked until she let hers fall shut and he closed the distance between them, his mouth sweeping across hers in a caress so gentle she nearly sobbed.

Some sound must have escaped her because his arms tightened about her and his lips crashed against hers, his hand gripping the back of her neck to keep her captive against him. Not that she had any intention of going anywhere.

If she thought the kiss down on the pier had been amazing, this one was...indescribable. Their first kiss had been exploring, heated, but controlled. This? This was frenzy, passion, desperation. A need so strong she shook with the force of it. They kissed with such a fury that their teeth knocked together, and she only vaguely registered it.

She wrapped both arms around his neck, one hand lightly scratching the back of his head. Her fingers would be tangling in his hair if he had any. Since that wasn't an option, she gripped the back of his neck so he couldn't escape her onslaught. Or maybe it was she who couldn't escape his. She didn't know or care. All she knew was that they were both wearing far too much clothing.

And...by some miracle she managed to dimly remember that there were far too many people about for her to straddle him like she really wanted to and rip his shirt from his chest.

"Oh my God, get a room!" Josh said.

Summer gasped and pulled away, staring at Garrett in a daze before glancing over at Josh and company.

Emily slapped his arm. "Why did you interrupt them? I wanted to see how far they'd get before they remembered they weren't alone."

Summer's jaw dropped, and the rest of the table burst out laughing.

"Oh, come on, Summer," Liam said. "We wouldn't have really let you guys go that far. Not that Garrett would have let you do anything you'd have regretted anyway," he said with a very pointed look at Garrett.

For the first time ever, Garrett's cheeks flushed red.

"Sorry," he murmured to her, nuzzling at her cheek. "Got a little carried away there."

She was going to tease him, but all it took was looking at him again, and the flood of heat that had taken over her rushed back.

"No apologies necessary." She tried to keep it together, but her already shaky breath hitched in the middle of it.

His eyes searched hers, and then he bit his lip and leaned closer so the others couldn't hear. "Where can we go?"

She didn't even have to ask what he meant. And for once in her life, she wasn't going to think it to death with pros and cons lists or friend polls or anything else. She wanted him. He wanted her. Any other thought in her head could take a flying leap. She'd figure out the rest later.

"My place."

He nodded. "As soon as the boat docks."

"Yes."

He let out a long, shaky breath. "Exactly how long will that be?"

She laughed and leaned her forehead against his. "Too long."

Chapter 12

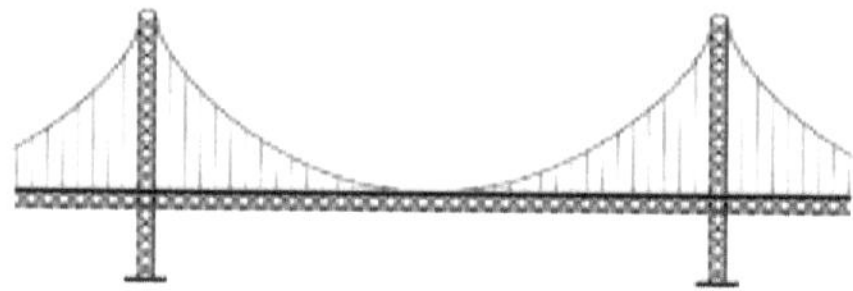

They had to wait another forty-five minutes before the boat docked. The longest forty-five minutes of Garrett's life.

They made sure they said their goodbyes as the boat was pulling in. And they were the first ones in line to get off. Pun not intended, but very, very apt.

Every one of their friends wore that amused and knowing grin that let them know they weren't fooling anyone. Not that they were trying to fool anyone. They'd spent the last forty-five minutes of the cruise pressed against each other while they swayed to the beat. Garrett had actually tried to be good. To keep his hands to himself. Because every touch stoked the fire that much hotter and by the time the dock was in sight, he was about ready to find a bucket full of ice to dump down his pants. That he managed to walk off that boat at all was a damn miracle.

His mind was so consumed with Summer and getting her alone that he didn't remember that neither one of them had driven there until they were off the boat and standing in the parking lot like a couple of lost puppies.

They both seemed to realize it at the same time and looked at each other, mouths open.

Summer laughed. "Guess we forgot a key detail."

Before he could answer, a car that looked like the one that had dropped Summer off pulled up in front of them and the driver rolled down his window. "Need a ride?"

"Joe!" Summer said with a huge grin. "How did you know?"

He shrugged. "I knew when the boat would be docking and took a chance that you'd need a ride home."

"You wanted to see how it ended that bad?"

He shrugged again. "It's been a slow night."

Summer grinned and Garrett looked at her, eyebrows raised. She nodded and he opened the back door for her to climb in before getting in after her. She sat in the middle instead of sliding all the way to her own side, and he grinned when he got settled and found his thigh plastered against hers.

"Thanks, Joe," she said.

"Any time, Ms. Laurent. Where to?"

"Call me Summer. And home, please." She rattled off the address again, and he nodded and pulled out of the parking lot.

As soon as they were in the car, Garrett took her hand again and began drawing lazy patterns on her skin with his fingertip.

"So how was the cruise?" Joe asked.

Summer sucked in a shaky breath and tried to answer like Garrett wasn't lighting up every nerve ending in her body. He smiled slowly as she shivered beneath his touch. People always neglected the classics. It was amazing what the brush of a hand could do. So much promise in such a small touch.

"It was great. Lots of fun," she managed to say.

Impressive. But if she was still capable of speech, he'd have to step up his game.

Joe nodded, but he kept his eyes on the road. "Yeah, I've gone on a couple with the wife. They've got that dinner cruise where you can go around the bay and have a nice buffet dinner. And a nephew of mine had a birthday party on one once and..."

Joe kept up a steady litany of words, but Garrett stopped listening somewhere between his nephew's birthday and his grandmother's knitting group's trip to Alcatraz. It was impossible to concentrate on anything with his hands on Summer. Even if it was only his fingertip.

He never would have imagined that drawing such a response from her from something so small and relatively tame, could be so erotic. Made even more so because they had to keep it quiet.

Why did subterfuge always make everything so much hotter?

He drew his patterns on the back of her hand for a few minutes, until her hand trembled beneath his. Then he let his finger trail up the inside of her arm, tracing the soft skin of her inner elbow before continuing its way up. To where her arm was pressed against her side.

He could tell when she held her breath, waiting, probably hoping, he'd move his finger to the side and explore further.

He leaned over, his nose brushing against the smooth skin of her cheek. "You doing okay over there?" he murmured in her ear.

"Fine," she said, though she had to try twice before the word was audible and when it came out it was still more like a choked whisper.

He chuckled, a low throaty sound that had her shivering against him again.

She shook her head. "I never in a million years would have imagined that I'd be sitting in the back of an Uber hoping a guy nearly a decade my junior would start feeling me up."

"Hmm," he said, his heart punching against his chest as his hands ached to do just that. "Yet here you are."

Her tremulous laugh had him sucking in a ragged breath. Who knew that sound could be so enticingly sexy?

But despite what she said, she wouldn't really want him doing anything in full sight of Joe the driver. However, there wasn't anything saying he couldn't keep being a little sneaky about it.

He trailed his finger back down her arm, his lips twitching when she nearly sobbed in frustration. He sympathized. And frankly was surprised she hadn't batted his hand away yet. Even for him, it was too intense. Too frustrating that he wouldn't, couldn't, go further just yet. And he wasn't even the one being touched.

But she didn't. If anything, she leaned against him harder. Urging him to do more.

***

Summer tried to sit back and be patient until they reached her house. They were almost there. Almost alone. And then they could do whatever they wanted to each other.

But it was like she was incapable of denying his touch. They'd been playing the longest game of foreplay *ever*. Taylor's idea of foreplay had been to grab the lube and spend thirty seconds or so applying it before rolling on top of her. She'd already been more aroused with Garrett in the last couple hours than she had the entirety of her marriage.

And she wanted *more*.

So, she leaned against him again, hoping he'd continue what he'd been doing. And bless the man, he seemed to know exactly what she wanted. He trailed his finger lower, drawing patterns on the bare flesh of her knee and her brain short circuited until the car pulled up in front of her two story, bright red, box style house.

"Here we are, Ms. Laur...Summer," Joe said, grinning at her in the rearview mirror.

Summer sucked in a shaky breath and hoped the smile she gave him didn't seem too strained. Social pleasantries were a bit hard to perform when her entire body was screaming for Garrett. She had never wanted—*craved*—anyone or anything as much as she did the man beside her just then. If she didn't get him inside the house and out of his clothes in the next three minutes, she might just start crying.

"Thank you, Joe." She opened her purse, but Garrett handed Joe a huge tip before Summer could.

"Thanks," he said to Joe with a smile.

"Any time, guys. Glad everything worked out," he said to Summer.

Then they were out of the car and up the steps that took them into the terraced backyard. To get in through the front of the house, they'd have to go through the garage, and it was a lot easier to go in through the back door. Plus, she really loved the back yard. Though the lush, terraced paradise was the last thing on her mind just then.

"This place is incredible," Garrett said, wrapping his arms around her from behind while she fumbled with her keys.

"Thanks. It belongs to a friend of Liam and Maggie's. The owner is very kindly letting me housesit until my house sells and I can get my own place. If we get our asking price, I might be able to afford a nice three hundred square foot studio."

Garrett barked out a laugh. "In this neighborhood? Two hundred square feet, maybe."

He wrapped his arms around her waist from behind and pressed against her, and she nearly dropped the keys.

"True," she managed to say while she fumbled to get the right key in her hand.

He nuzzled at her neck. "It was nice of them to let you stay here in the meantime."

Her breath released in a rush and the key scratched across the door handle. "Yeah."

He nipped at her earlobe, and she jammed the key so hard into the keyhole that she was surprised she didn't just punch all the way through the door.

"I'd love to see the inside," he said with a chuckle.

She choked out a laugh. "Me too. If I could just...get...the damn...key to work..."

He kissed her neck, and she damn near tore the door from its hinges shoving it open so they could stumble inside. Well, so she could stumble. Garrett sauntered in, his eyes burning into hers while he closed the door behind them.

She took advantage of the few seconds it took to deposit her purse and keys on the entryway table to try and catch her breath while he looked around.

Though she hadn't decorated the house, it was much more to her taste than her own home had been. This house was homey, comfortable, full of overstuffed furniture and warm earth tones. As soon as you stepped inside, it was like being wrapped in a big, fuzzy blanket. Comfortable and relaxing.

Usually. Right now, Summer was feeling anything but comfortable and relaxed. In fact, she wasn't sure what she felt. Might be excitement. Could be terror. It was like her body was playing emotion roulette, and she wasn't quite sure what it was going to land on yet. The only thing she was sure of was the desire coursing through her. Sheer, straight up, scorching hot lust.

What the hell she was supposed to do about it, she had no idea. Put the moves on him? Did people even say that anymore? They'd technically been putting the moves on each other all night, but now that they were alone, she had no idea how to get things to progress without just...jumping him.

Like she had the guts to do that. Ha!

She'd hadn't been a virgin when she'd gotten with Taylor in college, but she hadn't been far off. Their sex life had always been the one thing she'd thought they'd gotten right. She'd enjoyed it. Mostly. Even when the rest of their relationship started going downhill, they still seemed to do okay once they got in bed. Though, thinking on it now, they hadn't been very...adventurous. More like they'd known what worked and stuck to the classics. Nothing wrong with that. It got the job done.

At least, it had gotten the job done for Taylor. Summer had mostly just enjoyed the closeness. It was about the only time she had any physical contact with another human being. The fact that she rarely orgasmed—or that when she did it was so underwhelming, she usually took care of business later when she was alone—hadn't bothered her too much at the time.

It was becoming more and more evident that was because she hadn't known what she was missing.

And now here she was with this tall, dark, and panty-meltingly hot, young god...what the hell was she supposed to do with him?

She didn't know what would be worse. That a twenty-something guy wouldn't be as experienced as she was and need her to take the lead. Or that he'd be more experienced than she was despite having been on the planet for almost a decade less time.

"This place is great," Garrett said.

He stood in the middle of the room, his hands shoved in his pockets. Though despite what he'd just said, he wasn't looking at anything but her.

"Thanks," she murmured, her mouth suddenly dry.

He gave her that slow smile she loved so much and walked slowly toward her. She wasn't sure if he was doing it to be sexy, but, O.M.G., that slow stalking walk was off the charts hot. Or if he was trying not to spook her. Like some Australian wildlife expert narrating his actions while belly-crawling through the Outback...

There she is, the common mid-thirties divorcee, a timid creature who will spook at the slightest provocation. You must tread carefully when approaching...sneak up on her while her attention is elsewhere...quiet now...careful...now let's poke her with a stick...

A strangled laugh escaped her, and she slapped a hand over her mouth. Garrett raised an eyebrow but kept coming toward her until he was only a couple inches away. Close enough she could feel the heat rolling off him.

She put her hands on his chest and leaned her forehead against him, letting her hands slide down to his waist. He kissed the top of her head but kept his hands in his pockets, letting her come to him if she wanted.

"Sorry," she said. "Was just thinking of something really stupid."

"Oh?"

She glanced up at him and bit her lip to keep from smiling, though that didn't work. "Have you ever heard that comedian who pretends he's the Australian animal guy who stalks all those dangerous animals and then pokes them with a stick?"

"Noooo," he said, drawing out the word, though he was definitely amused.

"Ah. Well, you'll have to look him up, he's funny. Anyhow, when you were walking toward me, I just had that image in my head, and then the Australian commentary popped in and..."

His lips twitched. "And I was stalking you so I could poke you with a stick?"

"Yeah."

He laughed and finally took his hands out of his pockets so he could rub them up and down her arms. She kept her hands on his waist and dropped her forehead back to his chest.

"I promise if I poke you with anything, there will be plenty of foreplay first."

"Good to know," she said, bringing her hands up to cover her face.

"Hey," he said, pulling her hands away so she had to look at him. "Nothing happens unless you want it to, okay? We can keep making out or you can take me back to your bedroom and have your wicked way with me..."

She tried to cover her face again, but he laughed and held on to her hands. He kissed each one in turn and then bent down to make sure she was looking at him. "Or we can sit on that couch and watch a movie and do nothing but enjoy each other's company."

"You'd be okay with that?"

He gave her a gentle smile. "I just want to spend time with you. I mean, I'm not going to lie. I've got my fingers crossed you go for the bedroom option." He cupped her face in his hands. "But if you aren't ready for that, I'm down with whatever you want to do."

She took a deep breath and looked back up into his gorgeous brown eyes. She knew what she wanted. In fact, she wasn't sure how things had gone so downhill so fast just from walking in the door. "I've completely spoiled the mood, haven't I?"

He gazed at her for a second, maybe trying to gauge if she really wanted what she was implying she wanted. Though it was totally unfair to make him guess.

"I'd really love it if it wasn't spoiled," she added, and his lips drew into that heart-stopping half grin of his.

"I think we can probably get it back," he said, leaning down to kiss her.

That one touch was all it took. All the heat she'd felt before slammed back into her like it had been waiting in the wings for her to get out of her own head and let something incredible happen. His lips moved over hers and she clung to him, rising on her toes to give him better access.

He pulled away just long enough to ask, "Where?"

She started walking backwards, drawing him with her. After crashing into a second table, she finally gasped, "End of the hall on the right," and then went right back to kissing him.

Kissing him was all that mattered. She'd think later. Breathe later. All she wanted was to keep her lips plastered to his for the foreseeable future.

He picked her up and carried her down the hall. She had never been carried before in her life. Well, at least since she was old enough to reliably get herself from point A to point B. And certainly not since she'd packed on the extra weight during college. But he had her down the hall and into her room before any self-consciousness about what a heavy load she probably was could kick in. And if his heavy breathing stemmed from hauling her ass down the hallway instead of from the fact that they hadn't come up for air in the last several minutes...well, she didn't hear him complaining, so she was going to try not to worry about it.

He set her down and had his shirt unbuttoned and off before she could formulate a coherent thought. Not that him stripping helped her mental process any. Because just...*wow*.

She reached out and ran a hand down his chest, biting her lip when he trembled under her touch. His hands found the zipper at the back of her dress and slid it down. But she caught it before it could fall, her nerves kicking in with a vengeance.

"What's wrong?" he asked, his hands skimming up her back.

She sucked in a breath, her head swimming. And she wished she could shut off every other thought in her head and just let herself feel without any interference. But... "It's been a long time since anyone but...anyone else has seen what I've got going on," she said, refusing to say The Cockroach's name in this moment. "And the last woman you saw was probably some nimble twenty-year-old. That's a lot of perfection to compete with."

Garrett gave her that gentle smile of his that lit her heart up like a huge pile of Day Glo under a blacklight. He cupped her face in his hands in the way she was beginning to love. "When it comes to you, there will never be any competition."

She didn't even try to keep the skepticism from her face, and he reached out to brush her hair back from her cheek.

"There's no such thing as perfection, Summer. And if there is, then for me, it's you."

She shook her head, but she wasn't clinging quite so tightly to her dress.

"You are incredible," he said, kissing her forehead. "Do you have any idea how beautiful you are? You took my breath away from the first moment I saw you." His lips moved across her cheeks, down to the corner of her mouth. "You make me laugh. Just thinking about you makes me smile, and I haven't stopped thinking about you since the moment I walked into that house and saw you rocking out to that God-awful music."

"It's not awful," she murmured.

He chuckled, "Yes...yes, it is. But if it makes you happy, I'd gladly listen to it on repeat for hours."

She met his eyes, and he brushed the tip of her nose with his, just like Brendan Fraser had done in *Mrs. Winterbourne*. She trembled against him, and he drew her in even closer.

"There's a light in you that brightens my whole day. I just want to bask in you. All the time." He trailed kisses along her neck and throat as he spoke, finally moving back to her mouth. "If that's not perfection, what is?"

"You," she said, letting her breath out in a sigh. "You are absolute perfection. You couldn't be more perfect if I conjured you up in some *Weird Science* laboratory."

"Weird Science?" he asked with a slight frown.

She laughed. "We are going to have to sit you down and show you some 80's classics. These references are too good to be wasted."

He grinned. "Deal. But first..." He undid his belt and slid it through the loops, dropping it at her feet before he moved on to his pants. In a matter of seconds, he stood before her in nothing but a pair of boxer briefs that left absolutely nothing to her imagination.

She stared at him, her mouth going dry. He was her own personal Captain America, standing tall and proud before her, ready to be of service. Was she really going to let this once in a lifetime opportunity slip her by because she was self-conscious about a few extra years and a chub roll or two?

He raised an eyebrow, silently throwing down the gauntlet.

Your turn.

She took a deep breath. *All righty, then.*

And dropped her dress.

His breath left him in an audible rush, and his eyes lit up with a longing appreciation she'd never seen directed at her before.

"Good God, you're beautiful," he breathed.

If she hadn't been watching his face, she'd have never believed he meant it. But no one was that good an actor.

Their eyes locked and then he reached for her, his hands tangling in her hair and his lips were moving with a hungry urgency over hers. Then they were on the bed and there was nothing but him...his mouth, his hands, his tongue. Touching her everywhere, over and over until she was floating on a cloud of sheer pleasure. Had she really thought her sex life before now had been okay? It was like devouring a pint of Ben and Jerry's after never having eaten anything but the fat free, sugar free, dairy free, gluten free alternative her whole life. It might have scratched the itch in a pinch, but this...this was full of all the sinful goodness she'd never known she'd been missing.

And there would be no going back to what she'd had before after this. Nothing else was ever going to satisfy her. She was already addicted. She craved him, craved his touch. And he wasn't even finished yet.

He left her side for a second to grab a condom out of the pocket of his pants and quickly put it on before rejoining her.

"You still sure?" he asked, his lips trailing over her neck.

She shuddered under him. "I've never been more sure of anything in my life."

He moved over her. "Tell me what you need," he murmured.

She lifted her hips, showing him exactly what she wanted. He didn't make her wait. She threw her head back as he slowly filled her, taking his time so she could savor every moment until she couldn't stand it anymore. She needed more of him. All of him. She wrapped her legs around his waist, clinging to him as she rode wave after wave of sensation.

"Stay with me, baby," he said, holding her gaze until the rising crest inside her was too much to contain and she threw her head back, crying out as she shattered around him. His rhythm faltered and after a few more strokes, he followed her over the edge.

He held still for a second, both of them dragging in one ragged breath after another before he rolled to the side, taking her with him, their bodies still entwined while their hearts pounded in time together. He cradled her face, tilting it up so he could kiss her. And kiss her again. Before finally resting his forehead against hers.

He gathered her close against him like she was the most precious thing in the world and then kissed her shoulder before whispering a single word. "Perfection."

And that was it. Her heart shattered into a thousand pieces. Every one of them belonging to him. She was well and truly fucked.

Pun totally intended.

Chapter 13

"So," Liam said, scrutinizing Garrett enough that he had to clench his muscles to keep from squirming.

"So," Garrett said back.

"How's it going with you two?" He raised an eyebrow that pretty much said he already knew the answer but wanted to hear it anyway. "The last time we saw you guys you were fused at the lips and tumbling into an Uber."

Garrett couldn't keep the smile from his face. "We're doing great. I think."

"You think?"

Garrett watched Summer helping Emily dish up hot dogs for the kids. "She's amazing. And we're having fun. But I'm still not sure I can convince her to date me for real."

Liam laughed. "I'm pretty sure you *are* dating for real, whether she's admitting it or not. All you probably have to do is keep asking her to go places with you. I'd be surprised if she doesn't show up."

Garrett snorted. "Maybe. But it would be nice to be able to tell people she's my girlfriend or introduce her to my mom without her looking surprised. Or freaking out."

"Just give it a little while. You guys *did* just meet. She probably just needs some time to get used to the idea."

"Hopefully." He picked a piece of grass and absently chewed on it while he watched her with the kids.

She'd be such a great mom. Though from what he could tell she didn't seem real interested in that. Though...maybe that's just because she hadn't wanted kids with Taylor. But if she didn't want them at all?

Probably something he should keep in mind. He'd always envisioned himself with a houseful of kids. Not that they were anywhere near that serious. Yet. But still...was it fair to either of them to push so hard to start something that didn't have a future?

Was that even still the case anymore? Because he was starting to have an extremely difficult time picturing his life without Summer in it. But...he'd always wanted a family. The whole house, picket fence, family dog, bunch of kids running around scenario. For as long as he could remember, that's what he wanted. Was he willing to give that up if that wasn't what Summer wanted?

Liam's laugh broke his focus, and he glanced at his friend who was shaking his head. "You got it bad, don't you?"

Garrett's mouth quirked into a half grin. "That obvious, huh?"

Liam snorted. "Slightly. You haven't taken your eyes off her since you guys got here. Looking disheveled and exhausted, I might add."

The half grin turned into a full-blown smile. "Don't know what you're talking about."

"Uh huh." He shook his head again and jumped to his feet. "I'm going to get some food."

Liam passed Summer on his way to the food table, pausing briefly to say something that had her both smiling and blushing. Her cheeks were still faintly pink when she carefully settled herself next to him, somehow making sure the knee length sundress she wore was tucked in around her while she sat balancing a plate of food.

He hurried to take the food from her, leaning over to kiss her before he glanced down to see what she'd brought. The plate was piled high with hot dogs—fancy high-end hot dogs with fresh baked rolls, not the bargain brand he stocked his own fridge with—and a mountain of fresh fruit.

"This looks great," he said, kissing her again. And then again.

She laughed and kissed him one more time before grabbing a hot dog and sticking it in his mouth.

"I didn't realize until I got over there that I didn't know what you liked, so I just made the hot dogs the way I like them."

He bit off a huge bite. "They're perfect," he assured her, once his mouth was clear. "You can't beat a hot dog slathered with mustard." He took another bite and groaned in delight. "Wow. Now that's a hot dog."

She raised an amused eyebrow. "That good, huh?"

"Oh yeah. I'd share this one, but I don't want to."

She snagged her own from the plate, taking a bite almost as big as his own. He gave her a nod of admiration. Respect.

Her eyes rolled back in her head, and she put her hand to her mouth, nodding while she chewed. "Oh my God," she mumbled behind her hand, still chewing. "So good."

"Right?" He raised his hot dog in salute, and she followed suit, clinking hers to his like they were champagne flutes, before they both took another bite.

Garrett reclined on his side, propped up on his elbow while they plowed through the first hot dog, and each started on their second. There was only one left. And they were both eyeing it. He took a bigger bite and chewed faster. She noticed, her eyes widening, and did the same. He grinned and shoved half his hot dog into his mouth, and she slapped her hand over her mouth again, shoulders shaking with laughter as she tried to down the huge bite she already had in her mouth.

A shadow fell over them and they both looked up. Summer held up a hand to shield what sun was still hitting her from her eyes and the smile fell from her face. She finished chewing and swallowed hard.

"Taylor," she said.

"Summer." Taylor put his arm around Carolina's waist and drew her closer.

Summer smiled and nodded at her, and Carolina returned the gesture. Taylor seemed...disappointed. Garrett wasn't sure what the guy expected. Did he think they were going to get into some drag-out fight over him in the middle of the park? Summer was too classy for that, even if she cared enough to bother. Which she didn't. In fact, he was pretty sure she liked Carolina. A fact which must really irritate Taylor.

Garrett tried very hard to keep the scowl from his face while The Cockroach looked them over.

Taylor's nose scrunched in a grimace. "You have food on your face," he said to Summer, pointing to his own lip.

She glanced at him, more in curiosity, he was glad to see, than embarrassment.

"You have a tiny bit of mustard...I'll get it," Garrett said. He rubbed at the spot with his thumb before leaning over to kiss the corner of her mouth, darting his tongue out before his lips landed. Just to make sure he got it all off, of course.

Her breath hitched in her throat and her eyes were glowing with a sudden heat when he pulled away.

"Thanks," she said, her breathless bedroom voice making him momentarily forget where they were. Until Taylor cleared his throat.

Garrett pulled away with a sigh. That damn guy.

"I guess we'll see you tonight at the wedding," Taylor said, not meeting anyone's gaze as he turned to lead Carolina away.

Summer gave him a half-hearted wave, her attention never wavering from Garrett.

He gave her a slow grin that had her mouth dropping open in a breathless gasp. Then she bit her lip and his brain short circuited.

He leaned in...and then ducked a split second before a Frisbee went flying over his head.

"Sorry, Uncle Garrett!" Gracie said as she ran by with her brothers, chasing down their toy.

Garrett chuckled and watched them tearing across the grass for a moment before he turned back to Summer. "Good thing my Spidey senses went off or I'd have had a face full of Frisbee."

Summer leaned over to give him a quick kiss. "Spidey senses, huh? Are those Army issued?"

"Oh yeah. They pass them out when we graduate from basic training. Standard issue."

She laughed again and playfully pushed his shoulder before glancing over at where the kids were wrestling in the grass with their parents.

"I love them, but I don't know where Emily and Josh get the energy. Thank God I never had kids with Taylor."

Garrett chewed on his lip for a second. But...hell with it. Better to broach the subject sooner than later.

"Do you want kids?"

Her gaze shot to his, and he held perfectly still for a second before he forced himself to breathe and stop acting like she was a skittish horse getting ready to bolt. It was a reasonable question to ask someone you were starting to date.

She looked at him for a moment before glancing away. "I don't think so."

The disappointment hit him in the gut so hard he had to employ every skill he'd ever learned to keep it from showing on his face.

"I love kids," she said in a rush. "I just...I spend all day with them at school and I enjoy coming home at night and just relaxing in the quiet. You know?"

He nodded. "Yeah, I get that. But...you never thought of what it would be like to have your own?"

She shrugged and looked down at the grass she was pulling out blade by blade. "Sometimes, I guess. But I definitely didn't want them with Taylor. Even before things got bad. I mean, I watch Emily and Josh and they are both there and present all the time with the kids. Taylor would have been one of those fathers who thought his job was done once the sperm breached the egg."

Garrett nodded, a small kernel of hope in his chest. "But what if you were with someone else?"

She took a deep breath and finally looked at him. "I don't think so."

That last spark of hope died, but he kept his face blank as she continued.

"I know this probably sounds selfish, but I'm just starting to build a life for myself. When I was younger, I did what my parents wanted. Then I was in college, and I was dating Taylor and life revolved around what he wanted." She shrugged. "I'm finally free. I can go where I want, do what I want. I can pick up and move across the world if the opportunity presented itself. Kids are wonderful. And I know how rewarding being a parent can be. I see how happy my friends are with their children. But they are also tied down in a way that I don't want to be again. I just...can't see giving up that freedom when I've only just discovered it."

He nodded. "I get that."

She raised her brows. "Really?"

"Yeah, I do. I don't know, maybe it's because I've been on my own since right after high school. I graduated and was off to basic training a week later. And since then, I've been all over the world. I mean, I get wanting freedom, trust me," he said with a grin. "The Army has been running my life for a long time now. Not sure I'll know what to do with myself when I'm finally out."

She smiled but kept playing with the grass under her fingers. "You want the whole family thing though, don't you?" she asked.

He watched her for a second before he nodded slowly. "Yeah. I do."

The kids ran by shrieking with delight as Josh chased them with what looked like a bucket of melted ice, and Garrett and Summer both laughed.

Garrett finally shrugged. "I know it means giving up a lot. But that seems worth it," he said, nodding over at where the kids had hidden behind Emily who was playfully holding Josh off.

"I guess it's a good thing that this is just a weekend thing then," Summer said, her voice quiet.

Garrett turned back to her and had to suck in a quick breath at the stunning picture she made, her sundress fanned out around her, the sun glinting off the faint highlights in her hair. She looked like a damn angel with a body that was made for sin and soul that he knew deep down had been made to match his. The rest...would work itself out. He hoped.

"This isn't just a weekend thing for me, Summer. That hasn't changed."

Her forehead crinkled in a small frown. "But we want such different things."

He picked up her hand and smoothed his thumb over her fingers before he entwined their hands together and raised them to his mouth to press a kiss to her skin.

"Are you having fun with me?"

The smile that touched her lips was immediate, and her eyes lit up as she gazed up at him. "You know I am."

"Good." He leaned over and gave her a quick kiss. "Then for right now, let's not worry about anything else. It'll work itself out or it won't. In the meantime, we can enjoy being together."

She looked like she wanted to argue. But finally, she smiled and nodded. "Strawberry?" she asked, grabbing one from the plate and holding it up.

It was so not what he expected her to say. He blinked at her, his brain taking a second or two to catch up. He finally registered the fruit in her hand when she put it in her mouth and took a bite. He closed his eyes and groaned when her teeth sank into the soft flesh of the strawberry. He reached out to rub a hand up her arm and—

"Incoming!" Liam shouted.

They had half a second before all hundred pounds of Liam's golden retriever crashed into them in a whirlwind of fur, wagging tail, and slobbering tongue.

Summer shrieked when the dog slammed her to the ground, snatching the remains of the strawberry from her hand before he started foraging for more. Which unfortunately was on the plate between them. Garrett didn't even try to save the food. He was laughing too hard to do more than try and roll out of the way while the dog snarfed down anything remotely edible he could find.

Garrett crawled to Summer who had just about extricated herself from the ground. Until the dog decided to have a seat and planted his large furry butt right on her stomach.

"Oof," she huffed. "Get off me you moose," she said, pushing at him.

Liam made it over to them and pulled the dog off her and Garrett helped her to sit up, pulling her dress back down her thighs while he did.

"Thanks," she said, chuckling while he stood and pulled her off the ground with him.

"Sorry guys," Liam said. And he did look sorry, mostly.

Maggie and Emily ran over to them, Maggie holding handfuls of napkins.

"Are you okay?" she asked.

Summer laughed. "Yes. And thanks," she said, waving off the napkins, "but I'm pretty sure he got everything before any of it could land on me."

Liam shook his head and rubbed his hand over his face. "Sorry. He really loves strawberries. He saw you hold one up and..." He shrugged. "Sorry."

"It's okay," Garrett said, still laughing. He looked down at Summer and picked some grass out of her hair. "You good?"

"Yeah. No harm done." She looked down at herself and grimaced. "Well, maybe a little harm done." She chuckled. "Good thing we've got time to clean up before the wedding."

Now that sparked an idea. He caught Summer's gaze. "Yeah. In fact, maybe we should go do that now."

Her eyes widened but her lips twitched. "You're probably right. I mean, it might take a while and we don't want to be late for the wedding."

"Definitely."

Maggie's eyes narrowed. "But the house is just over—"

"Yeah, but we'll probably both need to shower again," Summer cut in, one eyebrow quirking up in either a challenge or invitation. Either way he was in.

"Oh yeah. For sure. We're filthy."

"Totally."

Emily snorted. "Oh, for God's sake, you two aren't fooling anyone. Go get your freak on already."

Summer blushed a little, but she didn't hesitate to take his hand when he put it out. "Get your mind out of the gutter. We just need to spruce up a bit." They started backing up.

Emily rolled her eyes, but she had a smile a mile wide. "Uh huh."

They turned and made a break for it before she could say anything else.

"Just don't be late for the wedding!" she called after them.

They might have thought to respond but they were too busy walking as quickly to Summer's car as they could without flat out running.

Chapter 14

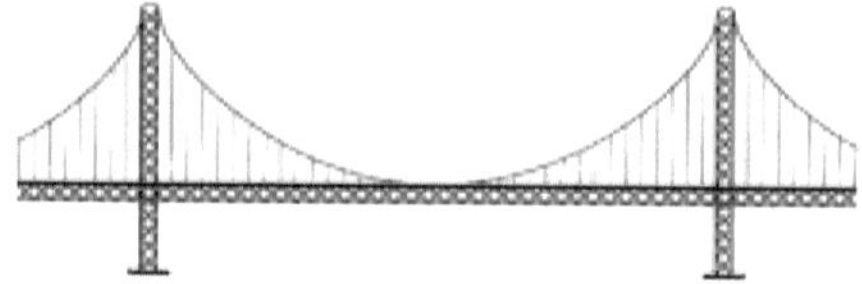

Two showers and several hours later, Summer and Garrett hurried across the street from the parking garage and up the steps of The Mint, pausing at the top to catch their breath. Well, Summer had to pause to catch her breath. Garrett looked like he could spend an hour running up and down those stairs without breaking a sweat. And that was after giving her four orgasms and enjoying a few himself. She didn't know where he got the stamina. Even when she'd been in her twenties, she would have found it hard to keep up.

"You could at least pretend like you're a little winded," she said, smiling so he'd know she was joking. Sort of.

He grinned. "Hey, you had to do it in heels. That ups the difficulty level severely."

She rolled her eyes. "You keep saying that. I might actually believe you one of these days."

He just laughed and wrapped his arm around her waist. "Come on, we're going to be late."

They'd barely made it in the doors and through the lobby when Maggie ambushed them. "There you are! We've got a wedding emergency."

She grabbed Summer's hand and hauled her down the hallway to where the bride was getting ready. Summer glanced back at Garrett who had followed them.

"Is it okay if he comes?" she asked.

"I don't care. Stay, come, just pick up the pace!"

"What's going on?" Summer asked, not sure if she should be amused or be worried.

Maggie pushed open the door to the room where the bride was getting ready surrounded by her bridesmaids. Most of them, at least.

"Oh! Summer! Thank God," Janine said, jumping up from her chair in a poof of tulle and lace. "Sandra and her daughter are home with a horrible case of food poisoning which means I'm down a bridesmaid and we have no flower girl."

"Oh no!" Summer said, squeezing Janine's hands. "What can I do to help?"

Maggie held out the fluttery soft yellow bridesmaid dress. "Sandra's about your size, so we were hoping..."

Summer's mouth dropped open and she looked from the dress to Janine's hopeful, stressed-out face, and back again.

"You don't have to do anything, just walk up the aisle during the ceremony and stand in for some of the pictures so we've got even numbers. And even that is negotiable," Janine said with an anxious wave of her hand. "But the ceremony...we can't have one of Tony's groomsmen walking alone up the aisle, and he doesn't want to ask one of them to sit out..."

"Of course not, I get it, no worries!" Summer said, reaching out for the dress. "Let's see if this baby fits."

Janine thrust it at her gratefully and pulled her into a hug. "Thank you so much!" She dropped onto a chair, blowing out a huge breath. "Now we just need to find a flower girl."

"I'm sure someone has a daughter who could do it, right?" Summer asked.

Maggie shook her head. "Not really. Most of the guests didn't bring their kids and the few who did have babies or children who are way too young."

"I'll do it," Garrett said, raising his hand with a huge grin.

Every woman in the room stopped and stared at him with their jaws on the floor. Whether it was because they had just noticed he was there or because the muscled-up Army Ranger had just volunteered to do a job usually handled by adorable little girls in flouncy dresses, she wasn't sure. Probably both.

"*You* want to be the flower girl?" Maggie asked.

He shrugged. "Why not? I'm old enough, I'd do a great job, and I look fabulous in flowers," he said, snagging the flower crown with trailing ribbons that was obviously meant for the missing flower girl and plopping it on his head. "If nothing else, it'll give the ceremony a memorable element of surprise."

Janine's mouth opened and shut for a second, like she was hoping if she made the motions the words would just come out on their own. Then she waved her hands with a laughing snort. "Ha! Fine, you're hired. I'll be the only bride in the city with a six-foot tall flower person. I love it."

Maggie took his hand, pulling him toward the door. "Okay, let me get you set up with the wedding planner. She'll tell you what to do."

Garrett winked at Summer and gave her a jaunty wave as Maggie dragged him out. Summer just shook her head. The man was insane, clearly. But damn, she loved that about him. Never in a million years could she have predicted those words coming out of his mouth. Dating him would never be boring, that was for sure. If they actually started dating for real. If he wanted that. If she wanted that.

Oy. She damn well knew she wanted it and if the past couple days had been even partially real, he wanted it to.

Was she brave enough to go for it? Was there a point in dating someone she had zero future with? Yeah, that was an entirely different question she didn't have time to figure out just then.

She wiggled into the bridesmaid's dress that was just a hair too tight across the chest. But all in all, wasn't too bad. The color looked great on her, the dress fell in soft chiffon waves to her floor, and thankfully, she'd worn her strappy nude heels which matched the dress perfectly.

"You look great!" Janine said when Summer stepped out from behind the changing screen.

Maggie bustled back in with the wedding planner before Summer could say anything.

The woman thrust a bouquet of flowers at Summer, eyes distracted as she listened to someone speaking in her headset, and then she clapped her hands with a huge smile. "Show time!"

She led the bridal party back down the hallway to one of the ballrooms that had been set up for the ceremony. The music started and the wedding planner started sending the bridesmaids and groomsmen. Summer's attention had been so focused on Garrett getting ready for his flower girl debut, she didn't notice that Taylor had come to stand beside her until it was almost their turn to walk up the aisle. How the hell had she forgotten he was one of the groomsmen? She turned a startled gaze to Janine whose draw had dropped.

"Sorry," she mouthed, looking truly stricken. Not a great look for a bride about to walk down the aisle.

Summer pasted on the happiest smile she could muster. "It's okay," she mouthed back.

She started up the aisle at the wedding planner's direction without bothering to look at Taylor, much less take his arm. Not that he offered it.

"I didn't realize they'd asked you to fill in for Sandra," he said, keeping his voice low enough only she could hear.

"It was a last second substitution," she muttered to him.

"Is your little boy toy really going to go prancing down the aisle with a basket of flowers?"

She rolled her eyes. "I believe he told you he prefers the term stud muffin. And yeah, he is. *And* he'll be fucking amazing at it."

Taylor's nose crinkled. "Nice language."

Summer pursed her lips together and bit down to keep from apologizing. Her stomach still clenched uncomfortably at the disgusted look on Taylor's face, and she had to keep reminding herself that it didn't matter if he was displeased. He couldn't make her miserable anymore unless she let him. Hopefully, one of these days she'd get that through her head.

They had reached the end of the aisle and Summer gratefully peeled off to the left to take her place with the other bridesmaids. Janine's maid of honor finished her walk and then it was Garrett's turn.

He started down the aisle, flower crown still on his head. Quiet laughter accompanied his march down the aisle as he took a step, stopped, and tossed a handful of petals in the air before taking another step. Every other step or so, he pulled a handful of flowers out and blew them off his fingertips at the guests who laughed and tried to catch them.

When he reached the end of the aisle, he waved his arm in a giant arc, showering flower petals down around him and the guests clapped for him. He took a bow and then came to stand beside Summer. The real flower girl probably would have sat on the floor near the maid of honor or something but thankfully Garrett didn't follow the plan that rigidly because that would have been a little too distracting.

Summer didn't pay attention much to what she was sure was a beautiful ceremony because it was impossible to focus on anything but Garrett. His hand straying across her lower back. Reaching down to lace his fingers with hers. The moment when the bride and groom exchanged rings and he rubbed his thumb across her ring finger. She tried very hard not to think about what silent message he was trying to send her with that gesture. Which was easier than it might sound because every time he touched her—hell, just the warmth of him standing so near her—short-circuited her brain.

His presence next to her was so overwhelmingly all-consuming she nearly missed the bride and groom kissing. Her cue to follow them back up the aisle. She gave Garrett's hand a quick squeeze and rejoined Taylor—who thankfully kept his mouth shut—for their recession back down the aisle.

Of course, that didn't last once everyone else had made it down the aisle and Garrett took his trip back down. On the way up, he'd kept it mostly professional. Now, with the ceremony concluded and everyone applauding and cheering the happy couple, he apparently decided to have a little fun with it.

He slid from one side of the aisle to the other like Tom Holland getting his Rhianna on, tossing more flower petals directly at the guests. Who all loved every second of it.

"You must be so proud," Taylor said, not quite able to keep the condescending sneer off his face. If he even tried.

The words were out of her mouth before she even had a chance to think about it. "You know, I never realized what an uptight twit you were when we were married."

If his jaw could have hit the floor, it would have. She had to clench her jaw to keep from freaking out herself. Apparently, it was a little easier standing up for Garrett than herself. She really needed to work on that. In the meantime, there was no way she was going to let Taylor say one solitary word against Garrett.

She just shook her head and tried to will her stomach out of revolting. "To answer your snide comment, yeah, I *am* proud. He's having fun and making people smile. Why wouldn't I be proud of someone who is bringing happiness to people? Maybe you should try it sometime."

Garrett reached them, and she didn't bother to glance back at Taylor to see if he had any response to her words. She couldn't give less of a damn what he thought about her or Garrett or anything else.

Instead, she took Garrett's face in both her hands and pulled him down for a heated kiss. "You were amazing, babe. The best flower person ever."

Garrett wrapped an arm around her waist. "Thank you," he said, pressing a kiss to her temple. "Everything good?" he asked while his lips where mostly hidden by her hair.

Her heart swelled with pride and affection for the man at her side. "Yeah. Everything's always good when I'm with you."

"Hmm." He wrapped his other arm around her waist to pull her in close and leaned down to rub the tip of his nose against hers. "I guess I'll have to make sure I'm always around then."

Her heart jumped, the sudden jolt of adrenaline his words caused making her tremble. A few days ago, even a few hours ago, she would have been certain it was fear making her heart race. But now...she wasn't so sure.

She wasn't ready for a commitment to anyone yet. Maybe ever. Then again, Garrett was an absolute dream come true wrapped in droolworthy package with the stamina of a god and the heart of a saint. She'd be a fool to turn down what he was offering. And she was many things but had never considered herself a fool.

But she'd never considered herself particularly brave either. And the things that Garrett wanted...she just wasn't sure they'd ever be on the same page about all that. Which made continuing to see him seem like a really bad idea. But the thought of not seeing him again was...well, unthinkable.

So, what would win out in the end?

Fear? Or what she very much suspected was the beginnings of love?

Hell, even she had no freaking clue.

Chapter 15

Summer sat at her table in the amazing courtyard of The San Francisco Mint, paying absolutely no attention to the gorgeous surroundings or the remains of the delicious dinner she'd barely touched—just the incredible man in front of her.

They weren't even talking. Just occasionally staring at each other while their hands softly intertwined, over and over again, their fingers softly sliding against each other. Such a simple movement. Such an innocent caress. One hand moving over another. Yet every brush of his skin on hers sent heated shivers running through her body, supercharging her already oversensitive nerves until she could barely draw a breath.

Had she truly thought one night with him would get him out of her system? All it had done was make her want him more. They'd made love more in the last two days than she had with her ridiculous ex during their last two years. And still she wanted more. She was starting to believe she'd never get enough. And that was terrifying. Thrilling. Exhilarating. But terrifying. Because needing someone that much, especially with the rather glaring opposite life goals they were already starting out with...it couldn't end well. Could it?

"What are you thinking about so hard over there?" he murmured to her.

She glanced up enough to meet his eyes briefly, then smiled and looked back down at their entwining fingers. "Nothing."

"That's not true." He bumped her chin with his knuckle, getting her to look up at him again.

She sighed. "Just thinking about the last couple days."

He gave her that slow grin that had her heart spinning like a Tilt-a-Whirl at a fair. "It's been pretty damn amazing."

She echoed his smile, unable to keep it from her lips. How was it possible to feel this happy? "I agree."

He took her other hand, threading their fingers together. "I don't want it to end tomorrow."

She took a deep breath. Jump or bail? Go for safety or give something amazing a chance? Despite the obstacles already in their way.

Her head said one thing. Her heart wanted her head to shut the fuck up.

She closed her eyes. And jumped. "Me either."

His smile was blinding, heart-shattering. He took her chin in his fingers and pulled her in for a lingering kiss.

"Marry me."

Her eyes shot open, and a surprised bark of laughter escaped her. He grinned but raised his brows in question.

"No," she said, shaking her head.

"Why not?"

Her eyes narrowed. "It's been two days."

"So, too soon?"

She laughed again. "A bit."

He just grinned. "Date me then."

"You want to date me? Even after everything we talked about earlier?"

He squeezed her hand. "I told you. I want to be with you. The rest…it'll work itself out."

"Issues like that don't just work themselves out, Garrett."

"Fine. Then we'll work on them together. But we can't do that unless we are actually *together*."

"It just seems like we are setting ourselves up for heartbreak."

He stared at their entwined hands and took a deep breath, letting it out slowly. "I learned a long time ago to take happiness where I could find it. Life is short. I've lost friends that I thought would be around forever." His shoulder lifted in a half-shrug. "I can't promise you we won't crash and burn. All I know is you are lighting up my life, and I want you to stay in it. Whatever comes down the road...we'll deal with it when we get to it. For now...let's grab some happiness. Date me."

Thoughts were bouncing around her head too fast to process them all. All the reasons she should tuck this weekend away as a great experience and move on with her life before she got hurt again when they inevitably broke up. And the utter depression that instantly struck at the thought of not seeing him anymore.

This was probably a really bad idea. Then again, she'd obviously made worse decisions with a lot more lead time. And this weekend had been the best of her life. She'd be a fool to just throw it away because she couldn't guarantee the future. Right?

She sucked in a slow breath. "Okay."

He flashed that brilliant smile again. "Really?"

"Yes."

"Exclusively? You're my girl?"

She hesitated for a brief second but then nodded. "Yes."

He clenched two fists like he was about to jump up and fist punch the air. But he contained it. Barely. She just put her hand over her mouth and laughed.

He pressed both fists to his own mouth and then leaned forward and pulled her hand away from her lips, kissing first her hand and then her mouth. And then he kissed her again, longer and deeper.

"You blow me away," he said against her lips, kissing her again.

She put her hand against his cheek, her thumb rubbing the space under his lip. "Garrett, I—"

"Summer, there you are!"

Her gaze shot up to the wedding planner. Well, Missy was actually the art teacher at their school, but she'd taken on the job as wedding planner for their headmaster. And had done an incredible job. Except now she looked completely freaked out.

"What's wrong?" Summer asked.

"Half the band bailed."

"What?"

"The drummer, keyboardist, and bass player are here, but apparently the lead singer and guitarist have the flu. They were going to try and make it anyway, but they just called and there's no way they can come. We're screwed. Tony and Janine are supposed to be announced for their first dance in five minutes and then the party is supposed to get started. The band has some replacements coming but they won't be here for at least half an hour if we're lucky. We need you."

"Me?" Her heart seized. "Why me?"

"Because you are the only one here with a halfway decent voice."

Garrett raised an eyebrow, but Summer shook her head. "No way, I suck."

"No, you don't. I heard you at the Christmas party."

Summer's jaw dropped. "That was karaoke, and I was passable at best."

"Well, passable is better than nothing," Missy said, turning her head to say something to someone at the other end of her headset.

"Missy, I can't—"

Missy sighed. "Summer, please. It's just a few songs."

"Can't we hook up someone's phone to the speakers or—"

"We tried. The stupid sound system uses some special kind of cable and doesn't have Bluetooth..." She broke off to listen to her headset again. "On my way," she said into it before turning back to Summer and grabbing her hand. "I am begging you. Just a few songs. For Janine and Tony. Come on."

Garrett stood with her. "I can play guitar if that'll help."

Summer looked at him in surprise, but Missy's face positively lit up. "Oh my God, really? You're a lifesaver. Again! Thank you!"

She turned, dragging Summer along behind her. Summer glanced at Garrett. "You play guitar?"

He just grinned and followed. "At least you won't have to be up there alone."

She released a pent-up breath, a smile breaking out despite the nerves clawing their way up her throat. She did feel slightly better. But only slightly.

Once they got on stage, Missy quickly introduced them to the three band members that had managed to show and then left to get the bride and groom ready.

Summer listened with growing trepidation at the planned song list. Garrett knew most of the songs or could fudge it well enough. But as for her...

"I don't know most of those songs," she said. "I mean I do, but probably not enough of the lyrics to make it all the way through the songs."

"Just pull them up on your phone and read them off that," Garrett suggested.

"That's..." She'd been about to protest but... "That's not a bad idea. Oh! Actually..."

She glanced around the room until she spotted Emily and Josh enjoying themselves silly at their table on a rare childless night. Hopefully Emily was still equipped with her normal paraphernalia.

"Emily!" she called, waving when a surprised Emily glanced up.

She hurried over and Summer leaned down to talk to her. "Do you have your iPad on you?"

Emily frowned. "It's in the car. Why?"

Summer sighed in relief. "Josh, go grab it for me, quick!"

The dear man didn't even question her, just took off running.

"What's going on?" Emily asked.

Summer filled her in while she went to the back of the stage where a bunch of extra chairs and a few music stands had been stashed. She grabbed one of the music stands and set it up at the front of the stage near her microphone. Sweet baby Bluebeard, she was really going to do this.

It was very possible her stomach was about to make a run for it.

She pressed a hand to her heaving gut and took a deep breath.

Josh made it back in record time and handed her a sticky but thankfully fully charged iPad.

"Thank you!" she said.

Emily and Josh wished her luck and went back to their table to watch what was sure to be the biggest shit show to end all shit shows.

She got the iPad ready with the first song and propped it up on the music stand.

Garrett, guitar strapped to his chest like the world's sexiest guitar player, nodded at her with a grin. "Smart."

She nodded back but blew out a long, trembling breath. She must have looked as bad as she felt because he stepped up to her, wrapped his huge warm hand around the back of her neck, and pulled her into a kiss that took her nervous breath away.

"Forget everyone out there," he said with a little head nod at the crowd. "Just pretend we're at some dive karaoke bar having a blast."

He winked at her and started strumming the first few chords of the first song.

Easier said than done, but surprisingly, watching him play that guitar was starting to take a lot of her nervousness away. It was hard to be too anxious when her entire being was too busy paying attention to her incredibly sexy boyfriend—holy hell, she was even thinking of him that way in her own head now. But...*dayum*.

Missy waved to her from over at the doorway and gave her a thumbs up. Here went nothing.

"Ladies and gentlemen, please welcome to the floor for their first dance as man and wife, Mr. and Mrs. Anthony Bolnicast!"

Everyone clapped as the bride and groom took the floor and the song started to swell.

Summer took a deep breath and fixed her eyes on Garrett strumming his guitar. His eyes burned into hers like he was promising her those hands of his would be moving over her the way they were moving over the guitar strings soon. She smiled and opened her mouth to sing.

***

A rush of pride hit Garrett as Summer stepped to the mic and introduced the wedding couple. No matter how nervous she was, you couldn't tell it by looking at her. The woman was badass. He really wished she'd figure that out.

Garrett strummed the opening bars of the song; thankful it was one he knew. He'd probably be googling sheet music in a few minutes if the replacement members didn't show up soon. Maybe they could just play the same few songs over and over again. If they kept the champagne flowing the crowd might not notice.

Summer opened her mouth to sing. The sound that came out...wasn't horrible. She wouldn't be winning any vocal competitions any time soon, but he'd heard worse. She turned anxious eyes to him, and he smiled and winked at her, nodding to encourage her to continue. And bless her brave heart, she grabbed that mic and gave it all she was worth.

By the time they started the second song, and the rest of the crowd joined the newly married couple on the dance floor, Summer seemed to have hit her groove. She still looked at him more than the crowd, but her voice was stronger and more confident the more she sang.

Garrett caught sight of Taylor once or twice. Of course, the jerk was standing with his arms firmly crossed across his chest like it would kill him if he pretended to enjoy himself for half a second. He was easy enough to ignore though since everyone else seemed to be having a great time. Except for the moment when The Cockroach rolled his eyes and laughed, leaning over to say something to the guy next to him. It was all Garrett could do to keep his ass on the stage when every cell in his body wanted to jump down and teach the asshole some respect.

The guy next to him just shrugged, said something in return that Taylor obviously didn't care for, and excused himself. Since that guy was on the dance floor grooving along with everyone else a few minutes later, Garrett could guess he didn't agree with Taylor's obvious disdain for the entertainment. Good. Asshat.

They started segueing into another song, and Summer quickly pulled up the lyrics on the iPad.

Garrett took the opportunity to lean over and give her some quick encouragement. "You're doing amazing! Keep it up!"

"You sure?" she asked, laughing though those gorgeous brown eyes of hers were still anxious.

"Look at them," he said, nodding at the crowd. "Are you having a good time?" he shouted out to the crowd.

Varying shouts of "yeah," "hell yeah," and other whoops and woots echoed back to them, and Garrett raised a brow at Summer. Then winked at her again and nodded to the microphone.

She took a deep breath and went back to belting it out. He could tell when she started losing her nerves and really got into it. Her voice grew even stronger, less tentative, steadier. She wasn't Taylor Swift, but she was shaking it off just fine. And when he joined her at the microphone to help with some backup, she turned a brilliant smile on him, leaning against him and singing for all she was worth.

He smiled back, singing along with her. And when the next song started, she started shaking the glorious curves her mama had given her. His girl absolutely wanted to have fun and he was *there* for it. Eat your heart out Cyndi Lauper.

By the time the replacement band members arrived, the party was in full swing, and his baby was *killing* it. He was a little disappointed they didn't need to keep going. Then again, with the actual band in place, he and Summer could hit the dance floor.

She gave up the mic with relief, though Garrett was pretty sure he detected at least a tiny bit of regret on her face. He took her hand and led her off the stairs at the back of the stage and then pulled her into his arms.

She threw her arms around his neck. "I can't believe I just did that," she said, breathless and radiant.

He grinned, wrapping his arms around her waist so he could pick her up. "You were amazing," he said, capturing her mouth in a searing kiss.

He would have loved to drag her off to a quiet corner somewhere and continue to show his appreciation, but their friends descended, all excited and exclaiming over what a great job she'd done. He stood back and let them shower her with admiration. She deserved every ounce of it.

"Thank you so much," Missy said, coming up to them. "That was amazing, seriously. I owe you big!" she said, running off again.

"Really, Summer, I didn't know you had it in you," Emily said. "I might hire you for Josh's birthday."

Summer chuckled. "Sorry, I'm retired. And you guys are sweet, but I wasn't that good. But!" she said, holding up a hand when they all started protesting. "I didn't suck. I'm happy with that."

They all laughed, and he threaded his fingers through hers. "Come on, baby," he said, walking backwards and crooking his finger, beckoning her to follow. "Let's dance."

He half-expected her to protest again. She didn't seem to enjoy putting herself out there. But she didn't hesitate.

"Absolutely," she said with a huge grin. "Take me to your dance floor."

He grinned. "Ah yeah, baby!"

He turned back around, draped her hand over his shoulder, and led her right to the middle of the floor, where they proceeded to tear it up like they were a couple of drunk sailors on leave for the first time in a year. Emily, Josh, Liam, and Maggie joined them and busted a few moves Garrett hadn't known they were capable of.

"I'm impressed," he said to Liam when he'd pulled a particularly tenacious move.

"Oh yeah? Watch this."

Garrett backed up, giving Liam some room to maneuver. He pulled a few moves that would have made John Travolta proud.

"Make room for the ladies!" Emily said, waving her hands at the guys to make a bigger hole.

She and Maggie, and to his complete surprise Summer, sashayed into the middle of the circle and started a coordinated dance routine that they'd probably been doing for years. They danced, kicked, spun, and grinded like a professional dance troupe, and Garrett was almost on the floor ready to worship at her feet by the time she crooked her finger at him to join her.

He didn't hesitate, dancing out to her with his heart in his throat.

She draped both arms around his neck, he grasped her hips, and they lambada'd their way across the floor. Every now and then he'd spin her, just to hear her laugh. But mostly, he kept her pulled as tightly to him as he could get her without it being totally indecent. Though the longer they danced the less he cared about decency. The woman could *move*. It was like she'd thrown every inhibition she'd ever had out the window and had just decided to live it up.

He didn't know what had possessed her, but as long as she took him with her, he was down for whatever came next.

Chapter 16

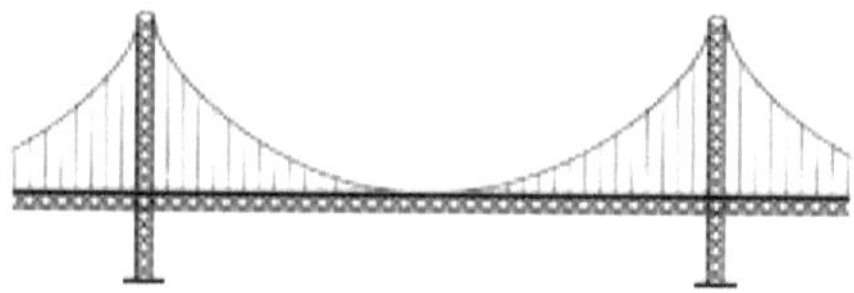

"Are you sure you want to do this?" Summer asked, looking at Garrett with her eyebrows raised in question. "This can't be fun for you."

"Are you kidding? I'm having a blast." He flashed her a huge grin and grabbed a shopping cart before heading into the Bed, Bath, and Beyond.

"You're having a blast? Following me around town while I shop for stuff for my house?"

"As long as I'm with you, yes." He leaned over and kissed her. "Now let's go get some linens and housewares."

He jumped on the back of the cart and rode it down the aisle until he had to stop or crash into a display.

She caught up with him and took over pushing the cart. "You'd really rather be running errands with me than laying on the beach back home?"

He snorted. "You know how hot it is in San Diego right now? It's way better up here. Especially because here is where you are. These are amazingly fluffy. You must get," he said rubbing a towel against his cheek.

She rolled her eyes but couldn't help but smile. They *were* very fluffy. She added four to the cart.

"But—"

"Summer." He leaned over the cart so he could get right in her face. "Why is it so hard for you to believe that I'm happy just spending time with you? No matter what we're doing?"

Her eyes searched his for a second, but she didn't see anything there but a genuine curiosity. She sighed. "I don't know. We've been together nearly constantly for weeks. Aren't you sick of me yet?"

"I will *never* get sick of you. I don't know why you don't believe me."

"Because...I mean...you're twenty-five, on vacation. You should be out living it up, not helping me decide if I should get a charcoal gray bathmat or go for classic white."

He shook his head and looked at her the way her mother used to when there was some basic life concept she wasn't grasping. "First of all, I've never been a guy who was big into 'living it up.' I'd rather stay home, cuddled up on the couch with my girlfriend and a good movie, than partying until I dropped with a bunch of strangers."

He brushed a thumb across her cheek and her heart turned to mush.

"Second, yes, I *am* truly enjoying helping you pick out things for your new house. One, because I'm excited for you. And two, because I find it pleasurable...," he leaned in closer and his gaze dropped to her lips, pausing long enough on that word to make her breath hitch in her throat, "to imagine all the ways we can use this stuff together."

"Really?" she asked, her voice hardly more than a whisper.

"Oh yeah," he said in his deep, bedroom voice that had her toes curling in her shoes.

"You've imagined what you'll do with this spatula?" she asked, grabbing the one she'd dropped in the cart.

The wicked grin he gave her had her knees going weak. "Absolutely. I can think of several things I'd like to do with it."

Her eyes widened.

He gave her a mock glare. "Get your mind out of the gutter. I was talking about making you some eggs or something."

Her cheeks flushed, and he leaned in again. "After an all-night marathon of intense lovemaking. Gotta keep your strength up. Also, might be handy for a good spanking or two if you're naughty."

Her breath punched out of her lungs with a surprised laugh. "And the towels?"

He didn't look at them, keeping his gaze locked with hers. "Drying you off after some wild shower sex."

"Hmm. I'm sensing a theme."

He shrugged and gave her that half-grin she loved so much. "I'm a simple man with simple needs."

She chuckled and closed the distance between them until their noses almost touched. "I think I can get on board with that."

"Best thing I've heard all day. Also, get the charcoal gray mat. The white would get dirty way too quickly."

"Done." She grabbed it from the shelf without even looking at it. She probably grabbed the wrong color. Hell, she wasn't even sure if she'd actually grabbed a bathmat. But there was no way she was going to rip her gaze away from Garrett to find out.

He dragged his teeth across his bottom lip in a slow sensual bite that had her body nearly vibrating with the need to have those lips moving over hers. She'd never been big on PDA, but in that moment, she wasn't one hundred percent sure she'd be able to stop from tumbling into a display bed with him.

She drew in a shaky breath and—

"I'm starting to think you're stalking me." Taylor's snide voice hit her like a bucket of ice water.

She and Garrett turned to look at him, and Garrett straightened up with a sigh. But he didn't say anything, stepping back as he usually did when they were confronted with her asshole of an ex. A flood of admiration and gratitude for Garrett hit her, bolstering her courage.

He could have thrown his considerable macho manliness around and chased Taylor off. Or gone all caveman and tried to stake some sort of territorial claim on her.

But he didn't. He hung back, a silent support ready to step in if she needed him, but otherwise, letting her deal with the situation the way she wanted, confident she could handle it. Which actually helped her feel the confidence she usually lacked around The Cockroach. She'd never had that kind of support before. And she was really getting tired of the person who should have given her that kind of support, and a world of other things, trying to make her feel bad about a relationship that, new though it might be, she truly valued.

From anyone else, that comment might have been a joke. *Ha, ha. We keep running into each other. We have to stop meeting like this. So crazy we bumped into each other again.*

From Taylor, it was cold, mean. An accusation. An implication she'd once again done something wrong and disturbed his perfectly ordered life.

And she was sick to death of it. Of him. Of their whole dynamic.

She'd hoped they could be the sort of civil exes who, at least after a period of time, could become friends. But it was really time to face the fact that Taylor had no interest in being her friend. Hadn't even when they'd been together. He didn't seem to have an interest in anything but continuously hurting her in any way he possibly could. And she'd put up with the little digs and snide comments long enough.

She took a deep breath and looked her ex square in the eye. "Taylor, we live in the same city. We have the same circle of friends. We like at least some of the same things. Chances are pretty good we are going to run into each other from time to time. But let me make this *very* clear. If we do happen to bump into one another, it will *never* be premeditated on my part."

Her gut churned and her brain screamed at her to stop before she really pissed him off. But she steeled her shoulders and pushed ahead. Enough was enough.

"Our divorce was final months ago, the settlement check has already cleared—thanks for being prompt with that, by the way—and our house thankfully sold in record time. The papers are signed; the lawyers will get our shares to us without any need for additional communication. There are no ties left between us to dissolve and nothing further we ever need to discuss. I will never purposely seek you out and have no desire to ever speak to you again. I will, of course, be civil if we ever find ourselves in the same social situation. Just as I would be to any stranger. But if you ever see me on the street or in a store, for example," she said, spreading her hands to indicate their surroundings, "especially if I am very obviously engaged in conversation with someone else—"

He snorted. "That's what you're calling nearly fucking each other in the middle of the aisle?"

Garrett stepped closer, letting her know he was there if she needed him, but he still stood back and let her deal with Taylor.

She wasn't even going to dignify Taylor's last comment with an answer. She continued like he hadn't spoken. "I want you to feel free to completely ignore me. You don't have to acknowledge me in any way, and you certainly don't have to speak to me. If I happen to meet your eye, a polite nod is fine if you feel the need. But I truly will not be offended if you just keep on walking. In fact, I'd prefer it. We are done. Let it go, Taylor."

Taylor's eyes were wide, whether with shock or anger Summer wasn't sure. And didn't care. She'd been wanting to say those words for so long now. The adrenaline flooding through her made her hands shake and she gripped the shopping cart to keep him from seeing it. But there was relief there as well. She couldn't control how Taylor might behave, but she'd finally said her peace. And God it felt good!

Garrett's hand slipped around hers, his fingers threading through hers and holding tight, and she looked up at him with a grateful smile. He brought her hand up to his lips and kissed it, his eyes bursting with pride for her. She was pretty proud herself. She couldn't believe she'd finally let it all lose and told Taylor off. And done it civilly enough, she thought. She had certainly had much more heated and expletive-filled mental convos with him in her darkest moments.

Hopefully, for once, he'd listen to her and just go live his life.

She was ready to leave the cart in the middle of the aisle, but when she looked back, Taylor was gone. She'd been so focused on Garrett, she hadn't even heard Taylor leave.

Garrett looked at her, cocking his head the way Liam's overgrown pooch often did. "How you doin' there? You good?"

She laughed, though it came out a little shaky. "Yeah. I'm good. Great, actually." She held out her free hand which was still trembling a bit. "Got a bit of an adrenaline crash going on, but other than that...yeah, I'm really good."

He pulled her to him for a bone crushing bear hug. "Yeah, you are, you badass. I really wish I'd have filmed that. The rest of the gang is going to be sorry they missed it."

She gave him a one-shouldered shrug. "It wasn't that big a deal. I just told him to leave me alone."

"Yeah. Something that wasn't easy for you and something that a lot of people never get the guts to do." He looked her up and down and nodded like he'd just made some huge decision. "Come on, let's go."

He grabbed the cart and took off down the aisle, keeping her hand firmly entwined with his so she had to hustle behind him.

She giggled. "Where are you dragging me?"

"To the bedding section. We need to get you some new sheets so we can take them home and do unspeakable things on them."

She picked up her speed. "I'm totally down for that."

Chapter 17

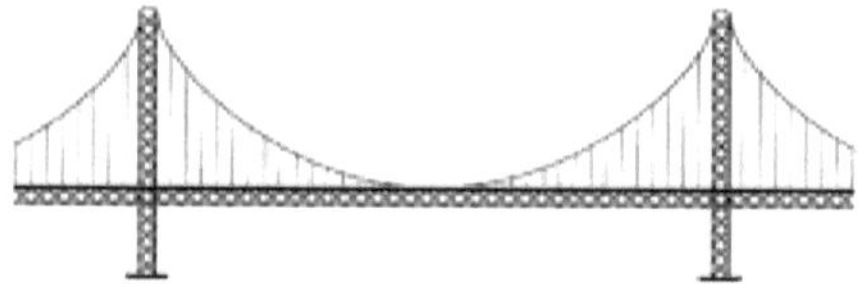

Garrett watched Summer go from one house to the next, her forehead scrunched while she worried her bottom lip between her teeth.

"There's no wrong choice, you know," he said, unable to keep from grinning.

She gave him an exasperated look. "Sure there is. It might look horrible in my house. Or what if I need something larger? Or smaller? What if I can't find anything else to go with it? I mean...it is kind of old fashioned."

They'd been perusing the offerings at the annual street wide yard sale near Summer's new house, finding odds and ends for her place. The table in question wasn't the newest model, for sure. But it was a beautiful, warm colored wood with delicately carved legs that curved toward the floor and ended in sort of curled, clubbed feet. The other table was much more modern, steel and glass with clean lines and sharp edges.

"Who cares what's in style right now? The only thing that matters is whether you like it."

She frowned at the tables again. "Well, this one is very similar to the one we had at the house," she said, pointing to the modern steel and glass table. "But this one..." She ran a hand lovingly over the surface of the wood table. "This one just feels warm and inviting, doesn't it?"

He smiled. "Any table with you sitting at it is warm and inviting. But warm and inviting seems a better endorsement than 'just like my old one.' Sounds like you prefer the wood one."

She nodded and took a deep breath. "You're right. Okay. The wood one it is."

"Good. Looks a lot sturdier too. That might come in handy."

She grinned and raised on her toes to kiss his cheek. "One-track mind."

God, she was adorable, all smiles and blushes.

He leaned down and gave her a quick kiss. "Guilty."

She just shook her head and kissed him back. "Thanks for putting up with all this."

"With all what?" he asked, giving her ponytail a little tug.

She shrugged. "You are literally standing in the street holding my purse. And you've been following me around, watching me try to make decisions all day."

"Are you kidding? Following you around is my favorite pastime. Although that makes me sound like a total creepy stalker."

That warm laughter of hers rang out and sent his heart pounding. It kicked up double time when she wrapped her arms around his neck. "You can follow me around any time."

"Excellent," he said, drawing her in closer. "In that case, I'm going to need some night vision goggles and a really good long-range camera."

She snorted and let go of him. "I guess that's better than you climbing in my window and watching me sleep at night."

"Oh, I do that too. Is that creepy?"

She snorted and shook her head. "You need help."

He nodded. "True," he said, winking at her. "And as for the purse..." He slung it around and pinned it to his chest so he could stroke it. "It goes perfectly with the outfit and has compartments for all my stuff. Anyone who has an issue with it is just jealous."

She pulled him down for a kiss. "You're too good to be true."

"Naw. You deserve even better than me."

She pushed away from him with a playful eye squint. "Agree to disagree."

He frowned at her but didn't argue again. For the moment.

She looked back at the tables. "I swear it wasn't this hard to decorate my last house."

No. It probably wasn't. Because as far as he could tell, all she'd done was buy exactly what The Cockroach liked without a thought to her own tastes. Making decisions based purely on her own desires was apparently a new experience for her.

"Hmm," she said, frowning down at her new table.

"Problem?"

"Gonna need some chairs."

He barked out a laugh. "Chairs would be useful. At least one. For me. Then you can just sit on my lap."

"Ha! Nice try."

He gave her butt a light swat. "All right, go find some chairs to go with the table. I'll keep an eye on all this stuff," he said, looking at the pile they were amassing.

It was a good thing they had Liam's truck. Hopefully the others weren't buying as much as he and Summer had. Of course, the others weren't trying to furnish a whole house, small though it might be.

"Be right back," she said, squinting at him again over her shoulder.

He was pretty sure she was trying to wink at him. One of these days, he'd have to show her how to do it right. Or not. The way she did it now was fucking adorable. He chuckled and stood back to enjoy the view as she sashayed off to find her chairs.

Then he caught site of a gorgeous floor lamp that she'd absolutely love. He spent a few minutes negotiating the price down and then paid a little extra for the guy to deliver the lamp to Summer's later that day. Definitely more than he'd wanted to spend but it would be worth it when she saw it.

A house a little farther down the street had a bunch of books sitting in front, and it was close enough that he could still keep an eye on their pile, so he went to check them out. Liam's birthday was coming up, and Garrett was suddenly inspired to get him an entire box full of romance novels. Which would be funny—no point denying that—but it would also be something Liam would enjoy. And it would give Garrett some new material to raid since he'd read most of the books Liam already had.

"Garrett! Hey man!"

Garrett looked around, grinning when he saw a group of his buddies heading toward him, a basketball under one of their arms.

"Hey, how are you? Haven't seen you in a while. Just get back in town?" Jay, a friend from his high school days said, giving him one of those sideways high five/handshake/fist bumps.

"Yeah, on leave for a few weeks."

"Awesome. We're going to go play a game or two, maybe head out for a beer later. You should come with."

"Ah, that sounds great, but I've got plans."

Sid—so nicknamed because of his uncanny resemblance to the cartoon sloth of the same name—jerked his head at the space behind Garrett. "Do your plans have anything to do with whoever is attached to those legs?"

Garrett frowned and looked over his shoulder. And then had to laugh.

Summer had apparently acquired two large potted plants and was barreling toward them, a plant in each arm, and little else of her visible but her legs.

"Yep, that would be her."

Sid nodded. "I approve."

"Glad to hear it," Garrett said, laying the sarcasm on thick.

"Hey, you had us scared for a minute there," Jay said. "I mean we *did* find you neck deep in the romance novels at a yard sale and covered in doilies and macrame."

Okay, they weren't wrong, but in his defense, it was much easier to carry the handmade plant holders if they were slung over his shoulders instead of in his arms.

He shrugged. “She likes plants.”

“And that?” Sid asked, pointing to the big floppy hat he’d forgotten was on his head.

He just grinned and pulled it off. “It’s pretty.”

The guys were wheezing with laughter by the time Summer reached them. Her face was lit up with excitement, so much so that she had barely come to a stop next to him before she was shoving the plants into his arms and excitedly chattering at him.

“Garrett, you’ll never guess what I found—Oh,” she said, finally realizing they weren’t alone. “Sorry, I didn’t mean to interrupt.”

“Naw, you’re good, babe,” he said, leaning over to give her a kiss before depositing her plants in the wagon they’d brought to haul their smaller treasures.

He introduced her to his friends, wrapping his arm around her waist when she tried to stand a nice platonic distance away. He knew she was still a little uncomfortable about their relationship, but she was his girl and he wanted everyone to know it.

She turned to him once they left. “If you want to go hang out with your friends, I totally understand.”

“I’m exactly where I want to be,” he said, pulling her in for another kiss.

“You’re sweet,” she said bumping him with her shoulder, “but really. If you want to hang out—”

“Summer,” he said, gripping her chin so she looked up at him. “I promise you, one of these days I’m going to want to go hang out with my friends for a while for a little guy time. And when the time comes, I will go with bells on. I promise. But today is not that today. Today, I’m all yours.”

He pulled her in for a kiss, and she melted against him with a faint whimper that had him digging his fingers into her hair with a groan. Her fingers fisted in his shirt, and she raised on her toes to deepen the kiss.

God, kissing this woman was like handling a live grenade. One touch and he was ready to combust. They needed to get back to her house and—

"Get him, girl," Emily said, coming up to them with a huge grin.

Summer broke away, leaning her forehead on Garrett's chest with a sigh before looking up to smile at her friends. Garrett chuckled and rubbed her arms. He knew the feeling.

"Em, leave them alone," Maggie said, though she was grinning.

Josh and Liam trailed behind them, arms full of odds and ends. Garrett's eyes narrowed slightly seeing that. They might need another truck.

"What were you trying to tell me a minute ago?" he asked Summer.

"What? Oh! Yes! We need to go up the road," Summer told him, ignoring her friends ribbing. "That gray house there, I bought a bed from them. A queen-sized, *brand new* Ikea bed, still in the box."

Summer sounded so excited though just the word *Ikea* sent a bolt of terror straight through Garrett's heart. But there was no way he was going to rain on her parade. And really, a brand-new bed still in the box was quite a score at a yard sale. So, he plastered on a smile and followed her to her new prize.

Ten minutes later and one bed richer, they met their group back near the truck and started to get everything loaded.

Emily looped her arm through Summer's. "Come on, lady. Let's let the men handle the heavy lifting while we grab your last few boxes from the house."

"Oh..." she said, glancing up at Garrett. His heart did its little tap dance that only happened when Summer was around, and he smiled down at her.

"Go," he said. "We've got this."

He jumped down from the back of the truck and drew her into his arms so he could whisper in her ear. "Maybe by the time you get back, I'll have that new bed of yours put together so we can test it out."

Her cheeks flushed bright red, but she gave him a smile that made his blood race. "Well, now I'm not sure if I should stretch it out so you have plenty of time, or if I should just scrap it altogether and we can ditch the bed."

He gave her a swift but searing kiss. "Go have fun. Get your stuff. You'll feel better with all your things under the same roof."

"True. All right. I'll go." She turned to walk away but looked back over her shoulder. "I won't be gone long though."

Her friends dragged her off laughing, and he stood watching her go, knowing he had the dumbest, goofiest grin on his face and not giving two shits.

Liam sighed and clapped a hand on his shoulder.

"Come on, Romeo. We could use some help with all this manual labor you just volunteered us for."

"For which there will be payback, just so you're aware," Josh said.

Garrett just grinned. "Worth it."

Josh and Liam just looked at each other and rolled their eyes.

"Oh, come on," Garrett said, picking up the wagon full of stuff and pushing the whole thing into the back of the truck. "Like you wouldn't do the same for your wives."

"Yeah, but Summer isn't your wife," Josh pointed out.

"Yet. She'll crack eventually."

The other guys both stopped and looked at him.

"You've proposed already?" Liam asked.

"Every chance I get," Garrett said. Then he frowned. "She keeps saying no though."

Jake snorted. "Maybe because you've known each other less than a month."

Garrett shrugged. "When you know, you know."

"What does she say when you ask? Aside from no," Liam asked, leaning against the truck with Josh while Garrett loaded the box with the Ikea bed.

"She mostly laughs. I don't think she thinks I'm serious."

Liam shook his head. "Yeah well, like Josh said, maybe it's because you've just started dating."

"You guys are real glass-half-empty type people, aren't you?" Garrett asked, carefully loading the table. "It's been almost a month since we met—which sounds much longer than saying less than a month, by the way—and that doesn't matter to me anyway. I know what I want."

Liam cocked an eyebrow. "I just hope you aren't rushing her."

His friend had their best interests at heart, but Garrett still scowled. "I'd never rush her. They haven't been serious proposals which is why she laughs them off and moves on." He pushed another box onto the truck and brushed off his hands. "Having said that, if she ever said yes, I'd be at the courthouse an hour later with a giant smile on my face."

Liam shook his head. "Just make sure you invite Maggie—"

"And Emily," Josh added.

"Or they'll kill you."

Garrett laughed. "Consider it done. Now, let's get this stuff to Summer's house so you two can unload while I watch *you*."

He jumped in the truck while they were still stammering protests of their innocence.

Chapter 18

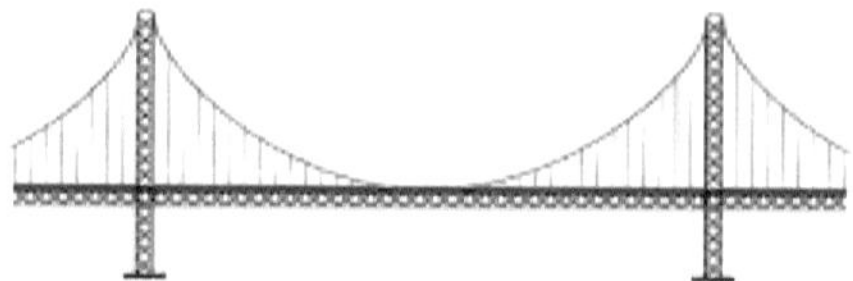

Summer sat with her hands wrapped around her mug of coffee while Emily and Maggie sipped theirs, watching her over the rims of their cups.

"What?" she finally said.

Emily glanced at Maggie and then back at Summer. "I think we're just waiting for you to spontaneously combust from happiness or something. I've never seen that particular glow before," she said, waving her hand in a circle near Summer's face.

Summer swatted at Emily's hand though she tried, and failed, to wipe the smile from her lips. "I'm not that bad."

Maggie laughed. "Fine, then stop smiling."

Summer smiled wider.

"I rest my case."

Summer shook her head and covered her face with her hands, growled a little, and looked back up. "It's ridiculous, isn't it? I'm acting like some high school kid. With a guy who is barely out of high school!"

Emily rolled her eyes. "Oh, stop. He's seriously not *that* young. And even if he is..." she said, heading off Summer's argument before she could make it, "he's very mature for his age. As cliché as that sounds."

"Yeah, maybe. But I saw the way his friends looked at me."

"And how was that?" Maggie asked.

Summer sighed. "Like they were a bunch of carefree twenty-somethings who couldn't figure out why their buddy was hanging around some old chick at a yard sale instead of slinging a few balls and beers with them."

"Oh stop," Emily said. "You're thirty-four, Summer. You're *not* old."

"Go ahead and tell me you didn't think thirty-four was old when you were twenty-five."

Emily blinked at her for a moment.

Summer threw her hands up in triumph. "See."

"Yeah, okay, maybe, but we were stupid. Thirty-four is *not* old."

Summer groaned. "I know that, and you know that, but some day Garrett might disagree. Like when I'm dying my grays and plucking chin hairs and he's still rocking a six-pack and wrinkle-free face. Or worse, even sooner, like when he wants to go hit a club at eleven o'clock at night and I'm ready for my jammies and a fuzzy blanket. Sidenote, when did eleven start feeling so late anyway? We used to party until four in the morning."

Emily snorted again. "It's all downhill after thirty. I swear, the second I blew the candles out on my thirtieth birthday cake my bones started creaking."

Summer threw up her hands. "See what I mean. He's still in that young 'anything-goes' range. I've hit that 'if it happens after nine, don't bother asking me to go' age."

Maggie scoffed. "Oh, come on. Give him a little more credit. He's not some typical kid who graduated from high school and partied his way through college. The military has a way of making you grow up fast. There's a lot of stuff Liam won't, or can't, talk about, but I know that he thinks really highly of Garrett, treats him like a real brother, trusts him with his life. Which Garrett literally saved a time or two. I mean, think about Garrett and The Cockroach."

Summer grimaced.

Maggie nodded. "See. You don't even have to think about which one you'd rather be around, let alone have around in an emergency or when life throws you a curve ball. You want someone you can count on and trust."

"Right," Emily said. "And having someone who makes you laugh and melts the panties off you with a single glance doesn't hurt either."

Summer choked out a shocked giggle. "Emily!"

She just shrugged. "Am I wrong?"

Summer put her hand over her mouth, but she shook her head. "No," she finally said.

"I rest *my* case," Emily said with a grin.

"But..."

"Yes?" Emily leaned forward, eyes alight with interest. Maggie wasn't quite as obviously eager, but she was just as curious.

Summer sighed. "It's just...he's always in a good mood. Like, *always*. No matter what happens."

Maggie frowned. "Is that a bad thing?"

"No..." Summer's forehead creased. "But it does seem...I don't know. Not realistic maybe? Not sustainable? I mean no one is that happy all the time. I guess I just keep waiting for the other shoe to drop. It makes me wonder what will happen when he does eventually lose his temper."

Emily shrugged. "Maybe he never will. Some people are just wired that way, where nothing bothers them."

Summer frowned. "Maybe. But it would still be nice to know if he's got a trigger and what it is. And how bad the explosion will be. It just sort of feels like if he's that happy all the time, maybe it's because he's the type who represses everything until it gets to nuclear explosion level."

"I get what you're saying," Maggie said, "but if it helps any, I really do think that's just the way he's built. Liam has never mentioned Garrett being anything but a good-natured, funny guy who everyone loves to have around. Maybe you're just too used to The Cockroach and having to walk on eggshells around him."

Summer considered that for a second. "Maybe. Probably. I mean, I know it's not fair to judge Garrett by my experiences with Taylor but..." She snorted lightly. "Hard not to."

"I know," Emily said. "But try. It's not fair to either of you to let The Cockroach murk things up."

"I know."

"And seriously, if your biggest complaint about Garrett is that he's too happy..." Maggie chuckled.

Summer had to smile. "I know. I'm pretty damn lucky, aren't I?"

They didn't need to respond. She already knew the answer.

And she tried to keep it in mind despite the nervous butterflies trying out for the Olympics in her stomach when she pulled up to her new house.

She sat in front for a minute, staring at it with what was probably a dopey grin on her face. Was it weird to feel such an overwhelming, visceral love for a house? Her heart literally skipped a few beats every time she saw it. And not just because the rent was actually decent (for San Francisco, at least). It was the polar opposite of her house with Taylor, though she hadn't consciously set out to find something so different. She'd just known this house was meant to be hers from the moment she laid eyes on it.

It was small, just one bedroom and one bathroom, compared to the four thousand square feet of her last home. And it was quaint and quirky and bright with its yellow siding and white trim. She loved the coral-colored door most of all.

Inside, the house was open, each room painted a different, vibrant, happy color. The purple living room would have had Taylor breaking out into hives. But Summer loved every square inch, even the quirky slanted ceilings in some of the rooms that came from squeezing every available inch of space out of the place. The attic was fully finished and delightfully bright and airy, and the house even boasted a small but gorgeously manicured backyard, complete with a new patio and lime and avocado trees.

It wasn't in a particularly fashionable neighborhood, but to her, it was a paradise. Just walking inside made all her cares drop away with a happy sigh.

Until she heard the cursing coming from her bedroom. She frowned and followed the torrent of expletives, her eyes widening when she peeked inside.

Garrett stood in the middle of the room, a screwdriver in one hand and what looked like an instruction booklet in the other, his face twisted with furious frustration. What little hair he had was standing on end like he'd been tugging on it and his look of abject irritation was so foreign for him that her mouth dropped open with a sound that was half-laugh, half-gasp.

She had never been so happy in her life to see someone so absolutely lose their shit.

He glanced up to see her standing there and thrust the instruction papers in her direction, giving them a good shake.

"There is no way in hell that these things are actually meant to instruct anyone on how to put this thing together."

"Problems?" she asked trying to keep the smile from her face.

He gaped at her. "Ya think?"

She clapped a hand over her mouth. It really wasn't funny that he was having such a hard time but...well...it kinda sorta *was*.

"I mean, this damn thing makes no sense! And it's not like I can't do this kind of thing. I'm good with my hands. I can assemble anything. Fuck, I can literally put together my rifle in under a minute *with my eyes closed*, but this shit? I mean, who the hell designed this thing, Satan?"

A laugh almost escaped, but she pinched it off with a snort. He wasn't paying attention to her though, too busy berating the pieces of wood strewn about him.

"I mean, this piece, the instructions say to attach this one to this one," he said, kicking at another piece, "but if you do that then the third piece—that little bastard over here," he said, flipping it off more than pointing at it, "won't fit. But if I put them together the way that it makes sense, then I can't get this one," he kicked at another piece, "to attach at all. So, you have to put that one on first but then those other two don't line up right."

He threw his hands up, letting the papers rain down around him. "I mean, what's so hard about just having two pieces of wood that nicely screw together? Why does there have to be a million little pieces that fit together in some weird freaking pattern that you need a fucking PhD in engineering to figure out and seriously I don't think even that would help. So now, I've just got a pile of useless of wood laying all around that we can't do anything with. You realize this is why that guy was so happy to sell this piece of hell-spawned furniture to you, right?

"Shit, he probably would have paid you to take it! I swear, I'm two seconds from dumping it back on his driveway and running like hell. I'll sleep on the floor from now on. It would be worth it. Seriously, so help me God, we are never buying anything Ikea again!"

That was it. She busted out laughing, unable to hold it back any longer.

His mouth dropped open, and he put his hands on his hips, which only made her laugh harder.

"My pain is funny to you?" he asked.

"No," she choked out.

He raised an eyebrow, which set her off again.

"Well, now, that's just not very nice," he said, tossing the screwdriver over his shoulder with a mischievous glint in his eye. He started picking his way through the debris, his eyes laser focused on hers.

Her amusement hitched in her throat, and she backed up, holding up a hand to keep him back. Though she couldn't keep the smile from her lips.

"I wasn't laughing," she said.

That eyebrow of his rose again, and he took another step closer.

"I mean, I was," she said, "but not at you. Just at the situation."

His other eyebrow rose, his mouth quirking into a slow half grin. A jolt of anticipation shot through her, sending her heart into overdrive.

"Not that the situation is funny," she said, still backing up. But her smiling mouth said otherwise. "It's just—" Her words ended on a squeal when he lunged across the remaining distance between them.

He wrapped his arms around her waist from behind and lifted her off her feet. She shrieked again and pretended to struggle...but not really.

His mouth latched onto her neck, and her laughter ended in a strangled gasp. She threw her head back, giving him better access while he carried her to the nearest wall and set her down facing it.

"Hands on the wall," he growled in her ear.

She obeyed immediately. "What are you doing?"

He ran both his hands up from her waist to her ribcage, dragging them over her breasts. "I'm giving you something to smile about."

He cupped her face, turning it back toward him so he could capture her lips, and she pressed back against him, trying to get closer. His mouth ravished hers until her knees turned watery. But when she tried to move her hands off the wall, he grabbed them and put them back.

"Keep them right there," he commanded.

She wasn't going to make any promises, but she was willing to see where this was going.

His hands dragged up her arms. One hand returned to her breast. The other traveled lower.

Okay. Keeping her hands on the wall had been worth it.

She sucked in a ragged breath when his hand slipped beneath her waistband. His mouth kept moving over the sensitive skin of her neck.

"Are you smiling yet?" he breathed into her ear.

Her laugh came out as more of a sob. "Not yet."

"Hmm, must not be getting the right spot then." His hand dipped lower, not stopping until he'd slipped two fingers inside her.

She threw her head back, her arms trembling with the effort it took to keep them on the wall. With the hard length of him pressed against her ass and his hands working their magic, her ability to keep upright was being sorely tested.

"Garrett," she gasped, trying to move against him, take his fingers deeper.

"I know, Gorgeous. Hang on."

She cried out in protest when he withdrew his hands, but then he was shoving her pants to the floor and pulling her shirt off before another sound could leave her lips. He spun her around and hauled her against him, grinding against her as he captured her lips again.

He walked her backward, giving her ass a good smack. "Unfortunately, there's no damn bed in this house, so the couch will have to do."

"Anywhere," she stammered, not caring where they went as long as his own pants disappeared quick.

He dropped to the sofa and pulled her down so she straddled his lap. Together, they made quick work of his jeans, her shoving them down until he could kick them off. They both let out a gasp when she sank down on him.

She would never get tired of this. Never. It wasn't just the feel of him inside her, though that was unlike anything she'd ever felt before. She didn't know if every other man she'd been with had been that bad, or if Garrett was just that good, but when he touched her, filled her, it was like he completed a part of her that she hadn't known was missing. Nothing existed for her but him as they moved together. And when that wave of pleasure finally crashed over, her gaze met his and she fell even harder.

With her ex, she'd kept her eyes squeezed shut, not wanting his face to distract her as she chased something she could never quite reach. With Garrett, she never wanted to shut him out. She wanted to see the heat building in his eyes, watch him come undone when she pulsed and shuddered around him. Every groan and gasp, every searing glance, every second of it she was storing away in her memory. Just in case.

Because no one would ever make her feel like this again. He was it for her.

And she still wasn't sure she could keep him.

"Stay with me, baby," he said, one hand grasping her hip while the other cupped her face.

She leaned in, her lips meeting his, keeping him captive until he found his own release.

He wrapped his arms around her and held her close.

And for a moment, it was enough. Nothing else mattered. Not their jobs, their ages, kids, cities...none of it.

She wished that moment could last forever.

Chapter 19

"Sorry about losing my shit back there," Garrett said, brushing Summer's hair back so he could kiss her neck in that spot she loved so much.

She smiled, snuggling back against him with a sigh of post-coital bliss. It was a bit of a tight squeeze spooning on the couch, but she didn't mind at all. The closer she could get to him, the better. "Don't apologize. I was relieved."

"Relieved?" She couldn't see his face, but she could almost hear his eyebrows raising.

She giggled. "Yeah." She turned enough in his arms so she could see him. "It's nice to know you're human. You seem a little too perfect sometimes."

He snorted. "Trust me. I'm nowhere near perfect."

She pursed her lips. "You're pretty damn close. It's a little intimidating."

His forehead crinkled. "So, you liked that I basically had a temper tantrum over some furniture?"

"Absolutely. You were grumpy. Cussing. Irrationally angry at inanimate objects. It was amazing, I loved it. I was starting to think you weren't capable of it."

He laughed. "Oh, trust me, I'm capable of it. I just don't sweat the small stuff. But that," he said, jabbing a finger in the direction of the bedroom, "is fucking torture."

"I'll help you," she said with a chuckle. "If all else fails, we can always hire someone to put it together."

He nodded. "Sure. Or we could just burn the damn thing and sleep on the floor."

She leaned back to kiss him. "As long as you're with me, I'll sleep anywhere."

"Really?"

"Really. On the couch, the floor, your place, my place, the beach, the car..."

"Are you going to get all Dr. Suess on me?"

She chuckled. "I might. Yes, I'll sleep with you in a car. I'd even sleep with you in a bar. I will definitely sleep with you here or there. I'll damn well sleep with you anywhere."

His eyebrows hit his hairline. "That was kind of spectacular."

"Thank you," she said with smirk, then leaned up for another kiss. "In all seriousness, though, I mean it. I just want to be with you."

His arms tightened around her. "I just want to be with you too."

She hugged his arms to her as he held her close. His lips trailed up to that soft spot behind her ear, and he placed a gentle kiss there. His breath tickled across her ear and she giggled and squirmed closer to him.

"I love you, Summer."

His words were barely more than a whisper, but they froze her in place. The only thing that moved was her heart and it was beating so hard it was nearly painful.

She could feel him holding his breath, could feel the disappointment in him when he slowly let that breath out a few moments later. Her heart hammered in her throat; her pulse so furious it made her ears hurt.

"It's okay if you can't say it back. I just wanted you to know how I felt."

He pressed another kiss to her neck and held her tighter.

She wanted to say it back. And not just because she didn't want to hurt him. She loved him too. At least she thought she did. But it was too soon.

They were so different, wanted such different things. Hell, she was a city-living, thirty-four-year-old speech therapist who was divorced and happily childless. He was still almost half a decade away from thirty, had some dangerous job he couldn't even tell her about, and wanted a white-picket-fenced house full of kids. That she probably wouldn't be able to give him even if she wanted to because even if they started making the first one right that second and got pregnant right away—hardly a given—she'd probably only be able to get two out before she hit forty. And that was if they barely left any space between them. That didn't sound appealing even if she wanted kids.

So how could it be fair to tell him she loved him? Would it be leading him on if she didn't think they had a future together? Would it hurt him more or less to know that she felt the same way if it wouldn't change things in the end? He was still young enough to believe in love conquering all. She was old enough to know better.

Maybe she'd already let this go on for far too long.

She rolled over to face to him, bringing her hand up to cup his cheek. "Garrett, I..."

He shook his head. "Don't," he said. "You don't have to say anything."

The tender smile he gave her nearly stole her breath, but the sadness behind his gentle eyes destroyed her.

Her heart clenched and her breath left her lungs with a sob, an overwhelming cascade of love for him driving her until she couldn't take it anymore. She pulled him down to meet her lips. They moved against his with a desperation she couldn't contain. The thought of him walking out her door and never coming back hurt so badly the pain took her breath away. She wrapped her arms around him and threw her leg over his hips, drawing him in and holding him captive. Like if she could just hold onto him hard enough, he could be hers forever, despite any obstacles in their way.

He must have picked up on her desperation because his hands and mouth moved over her with the same frenzy with which she touched him. And this time when he entered her, there was no playfulness, no giggling or joking. He stared into her eyes, like he was trying to imprint himself on her soul. But he was already there, firmly etched into the very essence of her being. She'd never be whole without him.

And when they finally lay exhausted and trembling in each other's arms, she pressed a soft kiss to his lips and found the courage to say what she'd been wanting to say almost since the moment they met. "I love you, Garrett."

He looked into her eyes for a moment, almost as if he couldn't quite believe what she was saying. And then a smile so brilliant it was blinding broke out. He gathered her to him in a rib-cracking hug. She laughed and held on for dear life. When he pulled away, it was only to kiss her until she was nearly senseless.

Somewhere in the outer reaches of her senses, she could hear a phone ringing. But it took several more minutes to really sink in.

She pushed away from him slightly, trying to elude his lips. "I think your phone is ringing."

"I don't care," he said, pulling her in for another toe-curling kiss.

"What if it's an emergency?" she said, half-heartedly. At the point, she wasn't sure if she cared if the whole world crashed down around their ears. As long as Garrett kept kissing her, nothing else mattered.

"No emergency is more important than worshipping the woman I love."

Well, if she wasn't head over heels before, that would have done it right there. Sweet Baby Hippo Fiona, she was done for. A total goner. Whatever may happen would happen, but she couldn't deny it anymore, that was for damn sure.

She sighed and lifted her chin to give him better access to her neck. "Let's just stay here forever," she murmured.

"Works for me," he said, kissing a trail down to her shoulder.

The ringing phone interrupted again, and she scowled in its direction. "It's probably Liam wanting to know where you are. Weren't you supposed to meet up with them again sometime today?"

"Probably. Don't care anymore. I've got more important things to kis...I mean, do."

She giggled again. "Good." She wrapped her arms around him tighter and arched into him. "I think I'll just keep you as my hostage right here all night. Maybe we can even get fully undressed at some point."

He chuckled. "Am I a hostage if I'm willing?"

She let out a happy sigh and nuzzled his neck. "I'm sure you'll want to leave at some point."

"Never."

She grinned. "Good. Because what I have planned might take all night."

He captured her mouth again, his lips moving over hers until her head spun.

"My plans are for much longer than that," he murmured against her skin.

"Hmm?" she mumbled, having a hard time latching onto anything coherent with his roving hands and mouth working their magic.

"I want to be with you..."

She gave him a soft smile, though the sudden intensity in his eyes had her sobering up quickly.

"Always," he added.

He sat up so abruptly he nearly dumped her off the couch. She braced herself and sat up, frowning when he quickly stood. The frown deepened when he dropped to a knee in front of her.

"I know this is fast, and I know I ask you all the time kind of as a joke although if you'd ever said yes, I'd have jumped on it. But this time, it's not a joke. I'm seriously asking. I love you, Summer. You are everything that is good and kind and happy in my life. I don't ever want to be apart from you. Marry me."

Her mouth dropped open. "Are..." Her mind spun out of control, trying desperately to process what he'd just said. A small part of her, in the back recesses of her mind, was clutching its heart and swooning over this wonderful man saying such amazing things.

The rest of her was overwhelmed with sudden, abject terror.

"Are you out of your fucking mind?" She jumped up, grabbing her pants and yanking them on. Somehow standing there half-naked made it all seem so much worse.

He raised an eyebrow in surprise, but she caught the flash of pain that he tried to hide.

She covered her face with her hands, horrified that she'd hurt him. "I'm so sorry. That's not how I meant that to come out, at all. But..." She let out an exasperated breath and looked back at him. "I'm sorry, Garrett, but really, what the hell are you thinking? You want to marry me? We've only been dating for like a month." She grabbed her shirt and yanked it on.

He shrugged. "What difference does that make? My parents dated for two weeks before my dad proposed, and they've been married for thirty years. When you know, you know."

She opened her mouth again but froze, completely unable to respond to that.

"Oh..." His eyes widened a little, and he looked down for a second, shaking his head with a small smile before looking back up. "But...maybe you don't..." He let out a slow breath. "I'm sorry. When you said you loved me too, I—"

She grabbed his hands, holding onto them like they were a lifeline. "I do love you, Garrett. I meant that. But...this is all still so new. Even if it feels like we've known each other forever, it really hasn't been that long. I mean, I knew Taylor for years before we got married and it still all went to hell. You're the first person I've dated since my divorce and—"

"So, I'm just the rebound guy?"

"What? No! That's not what I'm saying. I'm just...I just mean..." She sighed and raked a hand through her tangled hair. "I just think it's a bit fast. Don't you? I mean, you've never even really been in a long-term relationship."

"It only takes one if it's the right one."

"I know. I just..." She looked at him again, her heart breaking at the defeated look in his eyes.

"It's okay, Summer," he said, giving her hands a little squeeze.

She shook her head. "No. It's not. The last thing I ever wanted to do was hurt you. It's just...I'm just..." She pulled away from him with a frustrated growl and started pacing. "I want to be with you." She looked at him, her heart whimpering like it was being crushed in a vice. "I've never felt this way before. But it's..."

"Scary," he said, his calm, quiet voice shredding her to her soul.

"Yeah," she whispered, sinking back onto the couch. She took a deep, shuddering breath and looked around her new house. "I've never been on my own before," she said, glancing at him a little embarrassed. "Pretty sad for someone in their thirties, huh?"

"No," he said, in that same quiet, steady voice that had tears burning in her throat.

She shook her head. "I went from my parents' house to rooming with my college buddies to living with Taylor. This is the first time in my life I've really, truly been on my own. And I'm just not sure I'm ready yet to be a permanent *we* when I've never just been *me*."

He gave her a slow, sad smile. "I can understand that."

"I'm so sorry. I do love you, but I just can't..." She stopped and swallowed hard against the lump in her throat. "I know none of this is fair to you."

His forehead crinkled. "Who said life was fair?"

She gave him a ghost of a smile. "No one. But it's still not right for me to ask you to wait for something I might not ever be ready for."

Garrett looked at her for half a heartbeat and then shook his head. "You haven't asked me for anything, Summer. And what I'm willing to give isn't your choice."

"Garrett..."

His phone rang again, and this time Garrett picked it up with a frustrated sigh. Possibly because the damn thing had been going off for ten solid minutes now, but Summer suspected it was more to keep her from saying anything else.

But when he looked down at it, his whole demeanor changed. "Shit," he muttered, punching the screen to answer it while he grabbed for his pants and hurriedly redressed.

"Yeah," he said, his voice more agitated than she'd ever heard it. Whatever he heard on the other line had him straightening on sudden alert. "All right, I'm on my way."

He hung up, frowning. "I have to go." He leaned down, cupping the back of her head so he could kiss her forehead. "I'll try and call you later."

He spun and was out the door before she could draw another breath. She jumped up to hurry after him. "What? Wait! Who was that?"

He glanced at her over his shoulder but didn't stop. "Liam. My commander has been trying to get a hold of me. I'm going to get my ass chewed. I gotta go."

"What's going on? Go where?" She hurried down her front steps after him.

"I don't know yet." He climbed in his truck and then looked at Summer for a second before taking a deep breath. "We'll talk later."

"Garrett..." she said, but he was already pulling onto the street.

She stood watching until long after his truck had disappeared. Then she dragged herself back in her house, not sure if she'd just made the biggest mistake in her life, or if she'd just saved them both from making an even bigger one.

Either way, it hurt like hell.

Chapter 20

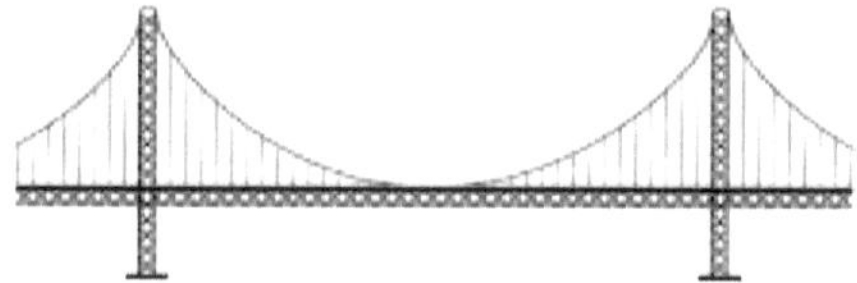

Garrett had only gotten half his duffle bag packed before Summer came crashing into his room.

He glanced up, the quick flare of happiness in his heart tempered by the anxiety that already boiled there, threatening to drown him. And not just because of the surprise deployment orders that had just come in. He was more afraid of Summer trying to break up with him than he was dying on foreign soil. At least if he was killed in action, his pain was over. If Summer walked away...

He swallowed hard and kept packing. "You waited a whole ten minutes before following me?"

"Seven," she said, closing the door behind her. "And a half." Her eyes moved over his bag and the pile of neatly rolled laundry he was shoving inside. Some of the fight left her, and she leaned back against the door. "You're leaving?" she asked quietly.

"Yeah. Orders came in."

Her eyes widened, the shimmer of a tear or two in her eyes. Unless it was a trick of light. "How long will you be gone?"

"I don't know. Probably six months. Maybe less if we achieve our objective sooner."

"Six *months*?"

He paused and gave her as sympathetic a look as he could muster. His family was used to not seeing him for large chunks of time. Though his mother still hated the surprise missions that came up. Well, she hated when he was gone no matter how much notice she had. But the surprise orders were the worst. Then again, they all tended to be surprise orders, even if he knew they were coming. He could sit around for months with his soft orders. Then one day hard orders for a completely different location would come in, and he'd be on a plane less than twenty-four hours later. One of the many reasons he was leaning toward not renewing his contract.

The other one was standing in front of him breaking his heart one little piece at a time. At least she didn't look like she was enjoying it either.

She swallowed hard and looked down at the ground. "And after? Will you come back here? Or I guess you'd have to go back home..."

"I still have a few weeks of leave left. I guess it depends on you."

Her gaze shot back to his. "That's not fair."

His lips quirked up. "I thought we'd determined that life isn't fair."

She snorted. "Understatement of the year."

"Do you want me to come back?" he asked, his pulse thundering in his head.

She took a deep breath and let it out slowly. "I don't think what I want matters."

"It does to me."

She shook her head, another strangled breath escaping her. "You know, I know you hate when I throw our ages around, but I'm sorry, it really does make a difference. In my twenties, yeah, it was easy to say screw it, let's go for it and who cares about the consequences. But now...consequences are real. They matter. And sometimes that means you have to make some hard decisions to avoid even worse consequences."

He gritted his teeth until his jaw ached. "So, you don't want me to come back."

"That's not what I'm saying. I'm just saying that maybe it's for the best...at least for now..."

He threw the shirt in his hand into the bag hard enough it would have torn through the canvas if there'd been more substance to it. "That's bullshit."

Her eyes shot to his, fire flashing in them. "You aren't experienced enough yet to unders—"

"Oh, don't give me that *I'm older and wiser* bullshit. I am aware you have a few years on me, but that doesn't make me some child who knows nothing of the world. When it comes to that shit, I think I've got you beat."

He came around the bed so he could touch her, unable to keep from doing so any longer. He grasped her upper arms, rubbing gently. "I get that you're scared, Summer. Believe it or not, despite my sunny disposition and endless optimism, so am I. I get that relationships aren't all sunshine and rainbows. Believe me, I've been in the military since I graduated high school, getting shipped out all over the world, away from the people I love. Trust me, I know how hard relationships can be. But that doesn't mean they're all misery and manipulation either. Just because you married one asshole and had a shitty experience doesn't mean we're all like that."

Her stubborn little chin jutted into the air. "I know that."

He frowned. "Do you? Because it seems like you've spent most of our time together using your ex as a great excuse to keep your distance."

She pulled away, that determined expression that he usually found adorable etched on her face. "Or maybe I meant what I said and just need some space for a while. Maybe this is moving too fast."

"Fast isn't always bad, Summer."

"No. But sometimes it is."

He straightened and shook his head, trying hard to keep from breaking down completely. "This isn't over."

He went back to his bag and put the last of his things inside.

"Garrett...you're leaving anyway. Maybe it's just easier to say goodbye, make a clean break—"

"No."

She flinched at his tone, and he took a deep breath, closing his eyes while he let it out slowly.

"First of all, it's never goodbye. Only see you later."

"Garrett," she said, her voice thick with emotion.

He sighed. "Look. Although I don't like to admit it, you do have a point about a few things. I am your first relationship since your ex. And while I don't think it always matters, it obviously matters to you."

He swallowed hard past the nausea that rose at what he was about to say next and just hurried and said it. "So, go date."

"What?" She jerked back a little in surprise.

"I'm sure of you. You need to be sure of me. And trust me, as much as I hate this idea, the last thing I want to be is your rebound guy. So, go date. I won't be here anyway. Get it out of your system if that's what you need to do. Just...keep the details to yourself, all right?"

He slung his bag over his shoulder and moved back to her. She didn't back away. He lifted his hand, slowly enough that she could move away if she didn't want him to touch her. But she stayed frozen in place, those big tear-filled eyes of hers tearing his heart into little shreds.

His thumb brushed across her cheek, and he leaned in to place a gentle kiss on her lips. "Just don't give up on us."

And then he opened the door and walked away, pretending he didn't hear her whisper, "Goodbye."

Chapter 21

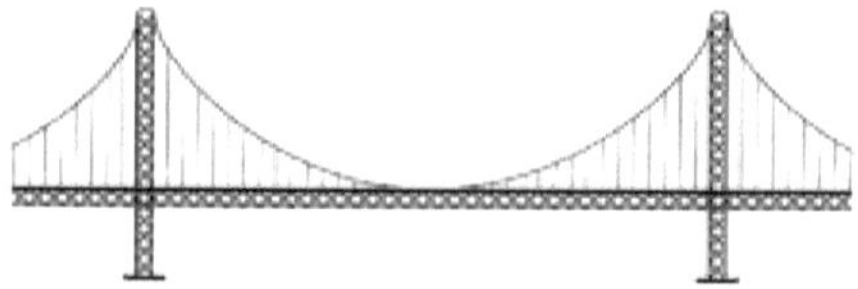

Summer's first month after Garrett left was a blur of misery and tears. The second ...wasn't much better.

School started up again, so at least she had something to do with her days. That helped a little. But it didn't keep her from jumping every time her phone rang. Not that she had any reason to expect he'd call. She wasn't even sure he could call from...wherever he was.

There was a slight sense of relief. Sort of like the feeling when something you've been dreading finally happens. The fact that it has happened sucks rocks, but at least the anticipation of it happening is gone. She'd been dreading losing Garrett since the moment she'd decided to let this thing...whatever it was...between them happen. Maybe even before that. Since the moment she met him. Getting involved with him was always a time bomb waiting to go off.

And now that it had...well, at least she didn't have to dread it anymore.

But oh, it hurt. So much worse than she ever dreamed. A thousand times worse than when her marriage had ended. That had broken her heart. But Garrett walking away had ripped the damn thing from her chest and shredded it.

He hadn't contacted her at all. No phone calls, video chats, texts, emails...not even regular mail. Nothing.

It's what she'd asked for. Space. But part of her really hated that he listened.

Or maybe he couldn't contact her. She had no idea where he was, what he was doing, when—or if—he'd be back.

And by month three, she couldn't take it anymore. She drove out to Liam's hoping maybe he'd be able to get some info for her. And maybe Maggie's shoulder would be available to cry on because she'd already saturated every surface in her house.

Liam and Maggie were at the front desk when she walked in. And by the glance they exchanged, they already knew exactly why she was there.

"We haven't heard from him," Liam said.

Summer deflated. She hadn't realized how much she'd hoped to get some small update until she heard those words. Even if she wasn't quite ready to talk to him herself, knowing what he was doing and where he was and if he was okay or not would have gone a long way to easing the turmoil inside her.

She sighed and Maggie shot a look at Liam again before coming over to wrap an arm around Summer's shoulders. "Come on, let's go sit."

Summer allowed Maggie to lead her into Liam's office where she slumped into the chair behind the desk with a sigh. Then she folded her arms on the desk and flopped her head down.

"I knew he wasn't exactly happy with me, but I figured he'd at least let you guys know his plans," she said, her voice muffled by her arms.

"He probably can't," Maggie said.

Summer lifted her head just enough to peek at her. "What do you mean?"

"That's just the way it is with some ops," Liam said from the doorway. "Everything is classified. Not even the families can know the details."

Fear stabbed at her, and she swallowed past the sudden lump in her throat. "I guess I knew that, but I just never thought..." She looked between Maggie and Liam. "So...we just won't know until he gets back?"

"Sorry, hon," Maggie said, rubbing her arm.

Liam's phone went off, and he glanced down at it. "Excuse me," he said, shooting her an encouraging nod before he left to answer his phone.

"So, what happened between you two?" Maggie asked.

Summer dropped her head back in her arms with a groan.

"Come on, you've got to give me a few details."

"She tell you what the hell is going on yet?" Emily said, marching in and plopping in the chair closest to Summer.

"Not yet," Maggie said, shaking her head with an amused grin.

Summer sat back and looked back and forth between the two sisters. She didn't stand a chance against both of them.

"How did you know I was here?" Summer asked.

Emily shrugged. "I didn't. I was on my way over anyway so it's just a crazy lucky coincidence. Especially since I was coming over so we could come up with a plan to make you snap out of it or talk or something. Glad to see you've finally left your house at least."

Summer frowned at her. "I like my house. I like being alone. I enjoy the silence."

"Yeah, well I don't blame you there," Emily said.

Summer's lips twitched. As a mom with three rambunctious kids, if anyone understood wanting to be alone, it was Emily. "I've never been on my own before, you know? Never lived alone. It's the first time I've really just been completely by myself for more than a couple days."

"And? Everything you dreamed it would be?" Emily asked, half-jokingly.

"Actually, yeah. I kinda love it. It's quiet, peaceful. Everything is set up how I like it, decorated how I like it. It's my space and I don't have to worry about what anyone else thinks or wants and it's the first time I've ever gotten to have a place that's just mine. I didn't realize how badly I needed something like that. Kind of like a little oasis away from everyone and everything."

"But?" Maggie asked. "Being out in the dating world not all it's cracked up to be?"

Summer snorted. "I've managed to go on three dates. They were all with perfectly nice guys that went rather well, and I have zero desire to ever call any of them again."

"Because..." Emily prompted.

Summer blew out a shaky breath. "I miss him."

Emily and Maggie exchanged a very similar look to the one Maggie had exchanged with Liam.

"Why do I feel like everyone is in on some inside joke but me?" Summer asked.

Emily smiled with a crooked half-grin. "It's not a joke, just a little insider info."

"Which is?"

"You're apparently the last one to realize you are in love with Garrett Vogel," Maggie said.

Summer covered her face with her hands and leaned her elbows on the desk. "Oh God, I know."

"Glad you finally figured it out," Emily said.

"I already knew, but it doesn't help anything," Summer said.

"Why?" Maggie asked.

"Because..." She took a deep breath and blew it out. "Yes, I love him." She ignored the excited look Emily and Maggie exchanged. "I do. I'm crazy, head-over-fucking-heels in love with him."

"So, what's the issue then?" Emily asked. "Because I'm pretty sure he feels the same way about you."

"He asked me to marry him. Like, seriously this time."

"He what?" the sisters asked in unison.

"I'm guessing you didn't say yes," Maggie said.

Summer shook her head, misery cascading in crashing waves through her. "I wanted to. Part of me did, anyway. A very big part. But..." She sighed again. "We haven't known each other very long."

"That doesn't matter," Emily said.

Maggie's forehead crinkled. "It helps. But sometimes...if it's right..."

"I know. But you know I haven't been divorced all that long. I feel like I've spent my life bouncing from one person to the next. Always needing someone there. And I finally get on my own, for real, and bam, I'm in love again."

"You don't think it's real?" Maggie asked.

"No, it's not that. Or not anymore. Now that he's been gone...What I feel for him..."

What she felt for him she couldn't adequately put into words. Just thinking of it overwhelmed her and made her heart pound so hard her head swam.

"It's real," she finally said. "But it feels like I'm finally figuring out who I really am. The real me when I'm not trying to make someone else happy. How can I mesh that with being in another relationship? Especially a relationship with a guy who wants different things out of life than I do. But then, how can I not?"

Emily sighed and reached over to take her hand, serious for once in her life. "Someone who truly loves you won't stand in the way of you figuring out who you are. They'll support you in the journey. I know you two haven't known each other that long. But I think you know enough. Is Garrett the type of guy who will throw roadblocks in your path? Or the type to clear the way for you?"

Summer shook her head. "He's the type that will stand by giving me silent support while I clear my own way because he believes in me enough to let me stand on my own. But will be there to help me with whatever I ask of him."

"I don't think you'll ever find a better partner than that," Maggie said with a soft smile.

"I know," Summer said, her heart and her head finally on the same page.

"So, what are you going to do about it?" Emily asked.

"I don't know. I know I'm not ready for marriage yet. I love him. More than anything. But honestly, I'm not sure I ever want to get married again. And he wants kids, and I don't. That's kind of a big deal. And he lives in San Diego and my job is here. And...oh my God, he has a job where I don't even know where he is or when...or if," she said, her breath strangling in her throat, "he's coming home. How do we reconcile all that? And if we can't—and seriously I don't see how we can—then I'll lose him and...I just don't think I can bear that."

Emily squeezed her hand. "People overcome all kinds of obstacles when they really want to make something work. You just have to work out a solution you can both live with. But that won't happen if you don't talk to the poor man."

"I know! But he's in some classified zone for some classified reason for some classified amount of time. How am I supposed to talk to him?"

"He won't be gone forever," Maggie said with an encouraging smile. "And he might not be able to contact you, but he can probably check his emails and messages at some point. Maybe just send him a quick note saying you want to talk when he gets back."

"Yeah," Emily said. "That way he knows you are at least open to negotiations."

Summer snorted. "Well, that's romantic."

Maggie grinned. "Come on. We'll ask Liam what the best way to contact Garrett is. Maybe he's got some strings he can pull or maybe he at least knows the best way to go about it all."

Summer blew out a deep breath and stood to follow the girls out of the office. Okay. She had no idea what she'd say to him. Or how they were going to figure out how to deal with all their obstacles. Or if he was even open to talking about them being a *them* after how they'd left things. But she wouldn't know unless she asked.

Now she just needed to figure out how the hell to contact him.

***

Garrett looked at Liam's slightly grainy face on his phone screen. The app they used to talk was great, being free and all. But the connection sucked so the visual quality left a lot to be desired. Then again, he was surprised he'd managed to get through at all, so he wasn't going to complain.

Liam shook his head. "You look like hell, man."

Garrett snorted. "That's why I always call you first. You keep me humble."

"Just doing my part."

Garrett's smile faded around the edges. "How's she doing?"

Liam didn't bother asking who he meant. "She's actually in my office right now crying on my wife's shoulder."

Garrett flinched. That's the last thing he'd wanted to hear. Yeah, he'd wanted her to miss him. He wanted her to want him enough to reconsider her whole breakup scheme. But he didn't want her hurting. "Is she okay?"

Liam raised an eyebrow. "She's not great. What the hell happened between you two anyway?"

Garrett sighed. "I asked her to marry me."

"Don't you do that like once a week?" Liam said with a frown.

Garrett gave him a sheepish grin. "Yeah, but I meant it this time."

"Ah."

"Yeah. She kind of freaked out a little."

"I bet."

"And then I got deployed right in the middle of the convo, and I haven't been able to call out until today. We didn't leave things on a great note. In fact, she kept trying to break up with me."

"Trying?"

Garrett's lips quirked up. "I sort of refused to acquiesce to her request."

Liam laughed. "Well, if it's any consolation, I'm pretty sure she doesn't want to break up with you. I think she's just scared. Taylor did a number on her."

Garrett tried to tamp down on the flash of anger that always hit him when Taylor was mentioned. That guy had the most amazing woman in the world and treated her like garbage. And continued to do so after leaving her. There weren't a lot of people that inspired actual hate in Garrett, but Summer's ex was definitely one of them.

"I didn't mean to push her," Garrett said, smiling when Liam's eyebrow quirked up. "Okay, maybe a little. But only because I know we could be so great together. I don't want to ever lose her."

"Marriage is no guarantee you won't lose someone," Liam said. "Summer has already learned that one the hard way."

Garrett frowned a little. "True." He shrugged. "I guess I just always had that image in my head...that idea of marriage being the endgame."

"Is it a dealbreaker for you?"

He frowned again. "I don't know, to be honest. I've never really thought of *not* getting married before."

Liam nodded. "I get that. But I guess you have to ask yourself what's more important. Being with the woman you love or being married to her."

Garrett considered that for a second. It really hadn't ever occurred to him they could be an official, full time, totally committed forever couple without a wedding. But...really it was the commitment part that was important, not the marriage part. How many marriages ended in divorce? More than half, according to most statistics. Making it official didn't seem to make it more likely to succeed.

He shook his head and snorted. "I want to be with her. However I can."

"Well then, there you go."

But Garrett frowned again. "She wasn't wrong about the other things though. We've got a lot stacked against us."

"Like?"

"She doesn't want kids."

"Ah," Liam said, nodding. Garrett didn't need to explain further. Liam knew how much he'd always wanted a big family.

"Is that a dealbreaker for you?"

Garrett took a deep breath and blew it out again. "If you'd have asked me a few months ago if this would be a dealbreaker for me in any relationship, I wouldn't have hesitated to say yes."

"And now?"

He shook his head. "The thought of not having kids makes me sad."

"Why does it sound like there's a but in there?"

"Because as sad as that makes me, the thought of not being with Summer..." Garrett had to stop and swallow past the sudden lump in his throat, his breath wheezing out of his lungs against the tightness in his chest. "It's unbearable," he finally managed to say.

Liam gave him an encouraging smile. "I think you two need to have a conversation when you get back."

Garrett choked out a laugh. "Yes, we do. Although it's not a conversation I want to have over the phone, and I don't know when I can get back up there."

"You still have some leave, don't you? Since your time was cut short?"

"Yeah, but I'm not sure—"

A loud bang and the eruption of gunfire sent a jolt of adrenaline rushing through him and he jumped up, grabbing his gear.

He glanced down at the screen into his friend's worried face.

"Tell her I love her," he said.

And then he ran out the door to join his team.

Chapter 22

One whole week. Seven days. One hundred and sixty-eight hours. Ten thousand and eighty minutes. That's how long Summer had to wait in absolute hell before Liam was able to find out that Garrett's unit was returning home.

But that's all he was able to find out.

They still didn't know what had happened. Probably never would. And worse, they didn't know if Garrett was okay. If he was coming home alive or...

Summer couldn't even make herself think of the alternative. Of any alternative but him walking off that plane.

It took another two weeks before they'd gotten word that his unit would be returning the next day. Garrett's parents were making arrangements to fly in but wouldn't be able to get there for a couple days. And still no one knew who, exactly, would be walking off that plane. Liam said no news was good news. But it was hard to keep that in mind.

Summer fidgeted in her seat for the thousandth time and Maggie—patient, kind, sweet Maggie—reached over and squeezed her hand and Summer gratefully clung to it. She couldn't begin to thank Liam and Maggie for coming with her down to San Diego. She'd have gone alone. Nothing was going to stop her from getting on that base to see Garrett when he arrived. But it was definitely a lot easier for Liam to get her on than her half-formed plan of trying to sweettalk the gate guards or scaling the fence or something.

But even Liam's contacts couldn't make the waiting easier. In fact, it was almost worse once they arrived on base. She had no idea when Garrett would show up, or even how he would show up. He could be flying into the nearby airstrip or arriving by boat or aircraft carrier or helicopter or hell, maybe he'd just swim up to the beach from the ocean all Bond-Girl-Halle-Berry style. Anything was possible and her mind concocted a thousand different scenarios while she waited.

It was extremely hard to come to terms with the fact that she couldn't just wish him there and have him be there. Even once he arrived, Liam warned her there would be debriefings and a bunch of other stuff she stopped paying attention to as he rattled them off. She didn't care about all that. She just wanted him back, safe.

She quietly snorted, and Maggie looked over at her. They were sitting in a lounge area, staring aimlessly out the window. Maggie silently supported her instead of trying to fill the silence with mindless chatter, which Summer appreciated more than Maggie would ever know.

"I guess the benefit, if it can be called that, of this whole situation is it pretty effectively cut through all my bullshit and got right down to the heart of the matter."

Maggie raised a delicate brow in question, not asking anything, just waiting for Summer to continue.

It took her a minute or two as she struggled to keep composed. "I don't care about whatever obstacles or differences we are up against," she said quietly. "If he won't be happy unless we're married, I'll marry him. Today. Nothing is a dealbreaker anymore." She glanced at her friend though Maggie's face was blurry through her tears. "Nothing matters more than him being here."

"Nothing?" said a deep voice behind her.

Summer gasped and jumped from her chair, spinning around to see Garrett standing in the doorway. He was leaning on a pair of crutches and looked thinner, his whole being exuding exhaustion. But he was there.

Maggie smiled and patted Summer's arm. "I'll leave you two alone." She gave Garrett a quick hug and then she and Liam left, their arms wrapped around each other.

Summer stared at Garrett for a few more seconds, her chest heaving as she tried to suck air into her constricted lungs.

Garrett just stood, his eyes roving over her in that eternally flirtatious way of his, his mouth quirking into that sexy half-grin she couldn't get enough of.

"Garrett," she breathed.

His smile grew. "Come here," he commanded.

She launched herself at him, throwing herself into his arms with enough force that he grunted. But he didn't push her away. He just chuckled and leaned against one crutch so he could wrap an arm around her and burying his face in her hair, holding her close while she completely and utterly broke down.

She clung to him, her body molding itself to his like they were two halves of a whole finally coming together to form a complete unit. They didn't say anything. Just held each other. Breathed each other. Took comfort from the familiar scents and feel of the other person's body. God, how did she ever think she'd be able to live without him? As utterly miserable as she'd been, she hadn't even realized the full extent of how empty she'd been until he was there, filling up her senses again.

"Told you you'd miss me," he said.

Her laughter left her in a choking sob. "Yeah, I missed you." She leaned her forehead against his chest, her hands fisting in the fabric of his uniform. "I missed you so much."

He kissed the top of her head. "Let's take this over to the couch," he said.

She looked up at him, horrified that the fact he was injured had somehow not completely registered.

"Oh my God, I'm sorry. Yes, couch." She hurried ahead of him, making sure his path was clear.

He sank down onto the cushions with a grateful sigh. Then she dragged over a chair and snagged a pillow from the couch so he could prop up the leg that was in an immobilizing brace.

"What happened?" she asked, sinking carefully down beside him on the couch.

He took her hand and she latched onto it, needing the contact. She breathed easier the moment their skin made contact.

"Broke my leg in two places. Tore a few ligaments."

"Oh my God," she breathed.

"I'll be okay," he said, drawing her closer to him so he could put his arm around her shoulders. "It probably won't ever be a hundred percent again. But the doc said I'll get most of my motility back."

"You don't seem too upset about it," she said, trying not to freak out though her heart was breaking for him.

He shrugged. "I always did love to prove doctors wrong. I'll be running circles around him before he knows what hit him," he said, flashing his brilliant smile at her.

She couldn't help but smile back. Then she wrapped her arm around his chest and curled herself into him, holding on for all she was worth. It could have been so much worse. His injury was horrible enough. But at least he was there, holding her. She was *never* going to take that for granted again.

"What's that?" he asked, nodding to a small box that was on the couch next to her.

"Oh." Heat flashed through her cheeks and her suddenly supercharged nerves sent the butterflies in her stomach into overdrive.

The idea for a little surprise package for him had seemed like a really good one when Emily had suggested it. Now that the moment was here though...

But it was now or never...

She picked up the box and held it out to him with a shrug. "Emily said I should bring you something."

He gave her an amused smile, his eyebrow lifting. "Emily and her deliveries."

Summer chuckled. "Yeah. I don't think she can help herself."

He opened the box and stared at its contents for a second. And then burst out laughing.

He pulled out the extra-large blueberry muffin with its rather unusual decorations. "Because I'm your stud muffin?" he asked, beaming ear to ear.

She nodded, her face flaming hot. It had seemed cute and funny when she and Emily had talked about it. Her relief that he liked it was so intense it made her feel a bit faint. The decoration though...she hadn't told anyone about that.

"And what's this?" he asked, pulling the ring pop off the top of the muffin. He cocked an eyebrow up. "Are you going to put a ring on it?"

She smiled. "I'll put a ring on anything you want as long as you stick around."

"Well, now, that raises some really interesting possibilities," he said, his smile softening into that dreamy bedroom grin of his.

He put the muffin back in its box along with the ring and then turned back so he could wrap his arms around her again.

"Thank you," he said, drawing her in close.

She tilted her head up, and he closed the distance between them, his mouth capturing hers in a kiss so tender and sweet she nearly sobbed.

"I love you," he murmured against her lips.

She threw her arms around his neck. “I love you, too,” she said, kissing him again and again. “I missed you so much,” she said, the words she’d bottled up inside for the last several weeks finally pouring out of her. “I kept trying to just go about my life, but I couldn’t. I was so afraid of so many things. Afraid we wouldn’t be able to work out our differences. Afraid our age gap would be a problem. Afraid it was too fast. Afraid of what people might think. Afraid of so many stupid, insignificant, pointless things. And then when Liam said something had happened...and we couldn’t find out any information...”

Her voice broke and Garrett pulled her back to his chest, his arm around her shoulders. He pressed her head to his shoulder, kissing the top of her head over and over. “Shh,” he whispered. “It’s okay. I’m here now.”

She nodded, clinging to him. “I’d been so afraid I might eventually lose you that I pushed you away. And then when I though I really had lost you...forever...I just...” She hugged him tighter. “Nothing else matters if we’re together. We can work out the rest. I don’t know how,” she said with a shaky laugh. “Maybe I can get a job transfer, or we can do the long-distance thing. The kid issue...”

“Isn’t something we have to figure out right this second,” he said, kissing her again.

She glanced up at him, eyebrows raised in question.

“I had some time to think things over as well,” he said. “There are things I thought I’d never compromise on that just don’t mean as much to me as I thought they did if it means you won’t be in my life.”

She frowned a little. “But I want you to be happy.”

“I want you to be happy too. And I know how simple and straightforward you like your life. Being with me...things are bound to get messy somewhere along the way. I don’t want you to ever regret...”

She brought her hand up to cup his cheek. “Do you think you’ll ever regret choosing me?”

“Never.”

A remaining tension she hadn't realized had been inside her finally released, and she let out a breath, giving him a soft smile. "As long as you are here with me, I am happy."

He turned his face so he could press a kiss onto her palm. "I feel the exact same way."

She couldn't stop her smile from spilling out, but she still worried that—

"Summer."

"Hmm?"

"Stop thinking so hard. We'll work it out."

She opened her mouth to argue, but instead she just smiled and leaned in for another kiss. "You're getting bossy in your old age."

He grinned. "Yes, ma'am." He kissed the tip of her nose and then let go of her so he could grab the box she'd brought. "Now, if you'll excuse me, I'm going to eat my muffin. I need to keep my strength up because I've just thought of several really nice places you could put that ring."

Damn, she loved how his mind worked. She'd been thinking the exact same thing.

Epilogue

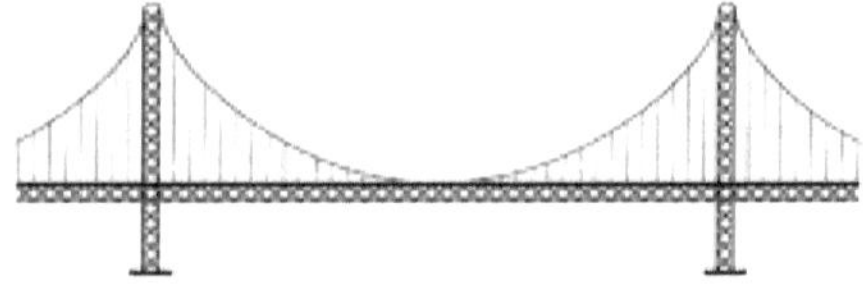

Summer stood bouncing her goddaughter on her hip while she watched Garrett romp through the yard with Emily's three kids close on his tail. They had behaved admirably in church, sitting quietly while Maggie and Liam's twins were christened. And their reward was chasing Uncle Garrett, Uncle Liam, and their father through the ninja courses until one of them dropped. Which, by the look of things, wouldn't take much longer.

Sure enough, five minutes later, the men stumbled out of the ball of dirt that contained the kids and headed for the refreshment table. And not a moment too soon. Little Emma started fussing for her mama, and Summer handed her off to Maggie. Who handed Emma's twin brother Brody to Liam.

Summer shook her head as Garrett wrapped an arm around her waist before downing half his Gatorade.

"Have fun?" she asked him.

He snorted and took another swig of his drink. "I don't know how Josh does it."

"I know, I was just thinking the same thing about Maggie. One baby is enough of a handful. I don't know how she's managing two."

"Let alone three who are old enough to run away from you," he said, nodding his head at where Josh was back to trying, and failing, to round up his offspring.

Summer laughed and leaned her head on his shoulder.

"You about ready to go?" he asked.

She nodded. "I just need to say goodbye to Maggie and Emily."

Emily heard her and came over. "Heading out?"

"Yeah, I think Uncle Garrett over here is ready for a nap," Summer said with a grin.

"Hmm, only if you promise to take one with me," he said, pressing a kiss to her neck.

Emily rolled her eyes, but Summer caught her smile.

"Oh, before you go, that package you were waiting for came in," she said to Garrett.

"Package?" Summer asked.

"Oh great! Thanks!" Garrett said. "Office?"

Emily nodded and he jogged off, only a slight hitch in his gait betraying his old injury. His leg had mostly healed up fine, but he still had some trouble with it occasionally. Especially if he overused it. He'd been contemplating not renewing his contract anyway when it was up, so when he was medically discharged, it hadn't been as horrible a blow as it might otherwise have been.

"What package?" she asked Emily again.

"You'll see," she said with a mischievous grin.

"I hate when you keep secrets."

Emily laughed. "Oh, relax. You loved the last package I sent your way. Or the delivery guy, anyway."

Summer looked back at where Garrett was just reappearing through the doorway and smiled. "Yeah, I do."

Emily glanced back and forth between the two of them and rolled her eyes again. "Seriously, it's been two years. When is the honeymoon period over?"

Garrett grinned as he came up to them, catching the last part of what she said. "Since she still won't marry me, I'm gonna say never."

Emily snorted then cringed at a particularly piercing scream from one of her kids. She went off to rescue Josh while Summer and Garrett gave their adorable godchildren a few more snuggles before climbing in Garrett's truck and heading back home.

The moment she walked in the door, she took a deep breath, relishing the instant calm that wrapped around her whenever she returned home. She still loved her little yellow house. It held more than a few touches from Garrett now that he'd been living there for almost a year. But she enjoyed seeing splashes of him intermingled with her own things.

They both dropped on the couch with happy sighs. Garrett wrapped his arm around Summer and kissed the top of her head. Then they both just sat and soaked up the silence for a moment.

There'd been a question nagging at Summer all day while she'd watched Garrett with the kids. She knew she probably shouldn't go poking holes in a perfectly working boat, but...she couldn't help but worry sometimes about what he was giving up to be with her.

"Are you still okay with your decision? About kids?" she asked, a small thread of fear worming its way into her gut.

He glanced down at her in surprise. "Where is this coming from?"

She shrugged. "Just from watching you with all the kids today. You'd make a great dad."

He slowly nodded. "Yeah. And you'd make a great mom. And I'm not going to lie, if you ever ended up pregnant, I would love our baby to the moon and back. But," he said, turning her face up so her gaze met his. "I am happy just the way things are."

"You are?"

The smile he gave her melted any last worry from her mind. And the kiss that followed wiped nearly everything else from it as well. She'd assumed that the heat between them would fizzle down the longer they were together. But it had been two years now and she still wanted to jump him like a show pony every time she was within six feet of him.

He finally pulled back and kissed the tip of her nose. "I am. Besides," he said, sitting back, "if I ever need a baby fix, our friends are keeping us supplied with a steady stream of godchildren who we can love on as long as we want and then hand back to their parents when we are done."

She laughed. "True."

"Plus, if we had kids, it would be a little more difficult to do things like this." He reached down near his feet and came back up with the package he'd retrieved from Liam and Maggie's.

Summer had forgotten all about it. But now... She tore it open and took a look inside...and burst out laughing. "What is all this?" she asked, gesturing at the boxful of *The SIDH* merchandise. Hats, a T-shirt, a water bottle, and a few other odds and ends tucked inside.

"Did you know that *The SIDH* is actually an Italian group?" he asked.

She cocked an eyebrow at him. "I did know that, yes."

"Huh. I found it odd considering the type of music they play."

"I guess...but you bought a whole box of their stuff for what reason?"

"Well, I was just thinking. If we lived there, I could take you to one of their concerts. And if you didn't want to live there, then at least you'd still have a bunch of their stuff."

Summer stared at him for a second, trying to let what he'd just said sink in. And when it did, her heart started ricocheting around her chest with the force of the adrenaline rush that hit her.

"Wait a second...are you asking me to move to Italy?"

Garrett's grin widened. "Not permanently. I know how much you love it here and I'd hate to be away from all our friends, and now Emma and Brody, for too long."

"Right. But?"

"But," he said, his hand moving up to squeeze her thigh. "My firm is opening an office in Italy and asked if I'd be willing to go and get things set up. It would only be for about a year, maybe a little longer. But you'd been talking about taking a sabbatical from work for a bit, so it seemed like a good time. I mean, I know it'll mess up your five-year plan a bit. Or a lot, depending on what happens down the road. And I know how much you hate your plans getting messed up, so I do, truly, understand if you don't want to. But, it is such an amazing opportunity so I didn't want to pass it up without talking to you. What do you say?"

Pick up everything and move to Italy with the man of her dreams? He wasn't wrong. It would mess up the new five-year plan she'd come up with after they'd become official. But she only had that plan because her old one had gotten all messed up when she'd met him. And the one before that had gotten messed up when she'd gotten divorced.

Maybe...maybe it was time to toss the plans out the window and just embrace the mess. Because it seemed to be working pretty well for her so far.

She grabbed Garrett's face and pulled him down for a searing kiss that left her breathless. Who was she kidding? It wasn't just the kiss. It was the man behind the kiss. Every glance, every touch, every moment she spent with him made her happier than the last. It didn't matter where they ended up. As long as they were together.

But Italy would be amazing for starters.

"I say yes!"

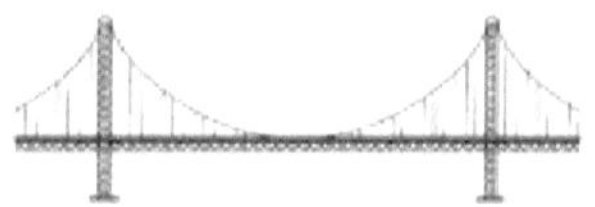

Acknowledgements

To my amazing support system, without whom I'd be a blubbering mess over in the corner: Lisa Rayne—you coming into my life when you did was a total godsend. And I dedicated this book to you for a reason because seriously, nobody would be reading it right now if it wasn't for you. Thank you for all the laughs, all the talks, all the plans, all the support...You are not only the wind beneath my wings, you are the one who superglued those wings onto my back and pushed me off the cliff. And for that I am eternally grateful.

Lexi Post, our monthly chats have become one of the highlights of my life and your encouragement not only in all my writing endeavors but in all other aspects of my life are so appreciated. Thank you for everything!

Toni Kerr, for everything you do for me, and all your years of support, I just can't thank you enough. Love you lady.

Jeanette—huge hugs and thanks for everything (also apologies for having to put up with me in real life). You have been my biggest cheerleader our whole lives and are always there when I need a sounding board or fresh eyes. Love you my sweet sissy.

And of course, to my amazing family who has to put up with me on a daily basis—my incredible daughter who takes care of me when I forget to take care of myself, I am so proud of your talent and your heart and your drive. I can't wait to see what the future holds for you. My truly awesome son, who is accomplishing things I can't even fathom and doing so with strength and courage, I am so proud of the man you have become. You are driven and strong and funny and kind. All your hard work is going to pay off in ways you can't even imagine. And to my sweet husband who drives me nuts but always knows just when to give me a hug or throw chocolate at me and run, love you, babe. You all make my world go 'round.

And to my readers—thank you so much for reading and reviewing and for all the emails and support. You all are just spectacular, and I couldn't do what I do if it wasn't for you!

Kira Archer is a jeans and t-shirt kind of girl who is addicted to chocolate and Goldfish crackers and spent most of her formative years with her nose in a book. She has degrees in history and English and is thrilled that she sort of gets to use them. Her novel Truly, Madly, Sweetly, was adapted as a Hallmark Original movie in 2018.

When Kira's not working, reading, or chasing her kids around, she can usually be found baking, diamond painting, or trying to find free wall space upon which to hang her diamond paintings. She resides in PA with her husband and two teens, the world's most spoiled dog, and a cat who absolutely rules the house. She also writes historical romance as Michelle McLean.

For more info on Kira and her work, please visit her website at kiraarcherbooks.com.

www.ingramcontent.com/pod-product-compliance
Ingram Content Group UK Ltd.
Pitfield, Milton Keynes, MK11 3LW, UK
UKHW041826200726
13854UKWH00002BA/606